THE ESSENCE OF MARKETING

The Essence
of Marketing

Bob Kimball, PhD

JAIN PUBLISHING COMPANY
Fremont, California

jainpub.com

Jain Publishing Company, Inc. is a diversified publisher of college textbooks and supplements, as well as professional and scholarly references, and books for the general reader. A complete, up-to-date listing of all the books, with cover images, descriptions, review excerpts, specifications and prices is always available on-line at **jainpub.com**. Our booksPLUS® division provides custom publishing and related services in print as well as electronic formats, and our learn24x7® division offers electronic course and training materials and development services.

This publication is designed to provide helpful information with regard to the subject matter covered. It is sold with the understanding that the publisher is not engaged in rendering legal, accounting or other professional advice. If legal advice or other expert assistance is required, the services of a qualified professional person should be sought.

All trade names of companies and products used in this book are trademarks, registered trademarks, or trade names of their respective holders, and have been used in editorial fashion only, with no intention of infringement of any kind. No such uses are intended to convey endorsement or other affiliations with the book.

Library of Congress Cataloging-in-Publication Data

Kimball, Bob.
    The essence of marketing / Bob Kimball.
       p. cm.
    ISBN-13: 978-0-87573-090-5 (softcover : alk. paper)
    ISBN-10: 0-87573-090-6 (softcover : alk. paper)
    1. Marketing. I. Title.
    HF5415.K51295 2006
    658.8—dc22

                                    2005034284

Printed in USA

CONTENTS

PREFACE
The Game Of Business Is Marketing

Talk to anyone in the business world today and you'll hear a common refrain: It's brutal out there. Competition was tough enough a decade ago when small businesses had to fight it out with their rivals across town, corporations were pitted against major domestic competitors, and individuals faced challenges from their peers and colleagues in the search for jobs and progression in their careers. Today, many business-people look to the past as the good old days. Now, in the global economy, competition comes from everywhere. Thanks to the Internet, customers can find any product or service at the click of a mouse, at a selling price less than your *cost.* Individuals discover, to their dismay, that there's someone, half a world away, willing to do their same job at a fraction of the salary.

Businesses large and small, faced with competitive pressures and eroding margins, are fighting for their very survival. Large corporations know that a disappointment in earnings can have disastrous repercussions on their stock price and the cost of borrowed capital. Small business people realize that a reversal of revenue and profit trends may signal the beginning of the end. And individuals awake to the reality that lifetime employment was an illusion and their very livelihoods are at stake.

It is understandable that businesses and individuals focus on financial results. The bottom line is the bottom line, after all. However, what many overlook is the fact that financial results—sales, profits, and income—represent only the scorecard, not the game itself. The game of business is marketing. Do the job of marketing right and financial results will follow. To a business, effective marketing is the difference between profit growth and Chapter 11. For an individual, effective personal marketing is the difference between gainful employment and the streets.

Think of marketing as something akin to a symphony orchestra with you its conductor. Every instrument is critical. The skills of each artist must be impeccable. And you must direct them to execute their roles in perfect synchronization. If just one instrument is out of tune or one artist off by half a beat, the entire production is ruined. But get it all right, and the result is beautiful.

Some business professionals equate marketing with the development and delivery of products and services. Others view marketing from the perspective of advertising, selling, and promotion. And many more perceive marketing as focused on production, pricing, and distribution. All those activities are elements of marketing, a section of the orchestra. All of those elements—and more—must be in place and working in synergy. In their totality, we have the essence of marketing.

Most of this book will concentrate on traditional business organizations that market products and services. However, the same principles apply to organizations that market ideas or advocate points-of-view, and to individuals who must market themselves to attain personal objectives. Now that you think of it, the game of life is marketing, too, isn't it?

CHAPTER I

Marketing Perspectives

Let's get started with a clear understanding of the terms "market" and "marketing." A "market" is defined as organizations or individuals, with wants or needs, who are willing and able to buy. Those wants and needs may be for a specific product or service—a ream of paper for the copier or a person to repair the leaky faucet—or they may be psychological needs that could be satisfied through numerous alternatives. For example, a middle-aged man wishing to reaffirm his youth and vigor might fulfill that need by purchasing a speedboat or embarking on a six-week adventure to climb Mt. Everest.

The fact that there is a market does not imply that someone will be available to serve the market. Yes, there may be qualified persons or businesses ready to buy, but if the market's potential is sufficiently small, no one may be motivated to address it. As examples, in many places you can no longer find anyone to do typewriter repairs. Mom discovered recently that there were no shocks manufactured to fit her Pacer wagon.

I routinely advise professionals to consider the job market they'll encounter. They would expect a large market for advertising and finance skills in New York City, but there might be no market for marine biology specialists in Oklahoma City. Many unemployed former executives are depressed at discovering that there is no longer a market for their middle management administrative skills.

If a market does exist, individuals or organizations may step forward, willing and able to supply a product or service that will address the wants or needs of buyers in the market. These suppliers are called marketers and their profession, aptly enough, is called marketing.

1

Marketing Defined

I've always thought of marketing as an organized system of activities designed to get the money out of someone else's pockets and into mine. However, the American Marketing Association (AMA) defines marketing as "an organizational function and a set of processes for creating, communicating, and delivering value to customers and for managing customer relations in ways that benefit the organization and its stakeholders." (Source: the AMA website, **www.marketingpower.com**).

Let's stick with their definition, the key term of which is "value." In a transaction, exchange is possible if each party has something of value to the other. The most obvious example is the exchange of products or services for money. You exchange your hard-earned dollars for a burger and fries to satisfy your hunger, or you go to the movies for some entertainment and relaxation. However, it is not necessary for money to change hands in the transaction. Consider the marketing activities of the major political parties. On one hand, their marketing activities are directed toward fund-raising. However, the ultimate transaction in politics is your vote. You spend your vote for the candidate of your choice in the same manner as you spend your dollars for the products and services of your choice. In return for your vote or monetary support, you attain the satisfaction of actively participating in something you believe will contribute to the realization of values or legislative objectives you consider important to your nation or community. As such, you are satisfying personal upper-level needs of personal fulfillment.

Let's take the concept of exchange one step further to consider a situation in which the transaction does not involve money in any way whatsoever. Social service agencies and not-for-profit organizations market ideas. Mothers Against Drunk Driving (MADD) implores citizens to act responsibly when drinking. The desired transaction occurs when a person decides that from now on he or she will leave the car keys atop the dresser and procure a cab to go out for the evening. In return, the responsible drinker attains a sense of fulfilling a worthwhile social obligation. Numerous organizations market the benefits of education, seeking the transaction of a young person electing to stay in school rather than drop out. In return, the young person attains a sense of purpose and esteem, all upper-level needs. Along similar lines, many community organizations employ marketing techniques to convince citizens to contribute time to programs that help the underprivileged. In addition to addressing warm-and-fuzzy esteem needs, volunteers get a line on their résumés that may enhance prospects at interview time.

The Four Marketing Management Orientations

Individuals or organizations can be classified as operating under one of four marketing management orientations. Generally, these philosophies have progressed over time, evolving from a predominance of the basic form in the past to a greater emphasis of the more advanced forms today. Let's take a look at them one at a time.

Form 1: Production Orientation

An individual or organization with the basic form, a production orientation, develops objectives and strategies from the perspective of what they want to do, what they do best, or what they can most easily produce. This philosophy, which was the norm a century ago, perceives competition to be among other firms in a generic product class, that is, a belief that there are no significant differences among competitive offerings. Thus, since a piece of lumber is a piece of lumber or a wool blanket is wool blanket, the firm's focus is on cost control and low prices.

Henry Ford was an example of a successful short-term implementation of the production orientation. His concept of the assembly line and product standardization ("You can have any color you want, as long as it's black.") propelled Henry to dominance of the fledgling automobile industry in the 1910s and 1920s. A production orientation is viable as long as product demand exceeds supply but it leaves a firm vulnerable to a competitor who offers a differentiated product with features the market is willing to pay for. Henry discovered this the hard way, and Ford has never regained its #1 position in the industry.

Numerous individuals and organizations persist with a production orientation to this day, some successfully, some not so successfully. On the not-so-successful end of the scale, Crystal Goblett recently opened a restaurant in town because, she said, "There's no place around here where you can get high-class international cuisine."

"Perhaps the reason for that," I suggested, "is that our idea of gourmet dining is the Sunday buffet at the Thunder Road Truck Stop out by the Interstate." She was in business less than a month before going belly-up.

Faye Dowdey is one of Mom's neighbors at the Camellia Gardens Trailer Park and Rest Home, just down the road from my place. Faye's hobby is making bird feeders, which she sells at their gift shop. She gets along pretty well on Social Security and makes the bird feeders mostly because it's something she loves to do. It also provides her with some "mad money" for joining the Goodtimers on their monthly bus trip to Biloxi to enjoy a show and spend a couple of hours working the nickel slot machines. Faye makes and sells about three bird feeders a month, and so far business is pretty good. However, she may face the possibility of reaching the total sales potential of the gift shop's target market. Additionally, the new Wal-Mart also sells bird feeders, just as nice as Faye's, at half her price. Faye may face a future in which she can only join the Goodtimers every other month.

An example of a successful production orientation, in a service business, is Ted Tinker, who repairs antique clocks. Ted is the only guy around here who does this and business is booming. Ted is no fool and knows enough about economics to raise his prices by five bucks an hour every time his backlog of work exceeds 90 days. I've got several old clocks around the place and periodically one of them needs attention. I contacted Ted recently and he told me, "It'll be about four months before I can get to it. I'll put you on the list and give you a call." Ted has no competition and says he's amazed young craftsmen seem disinterested in getting into the trade. Ted's commanding sixty dollars an hour now and there appears to be no end in sight.

Production orientation had a renaissance during World War II as the American industrial machine cranked out all the planes, ships, and materiel needed to lead the allies to victory. It remained viable in the immediate postwar years as industry transformed to a peacetime economy to supply consumer goods that had not been produced during the war. GE had an anxious buyer for every washing machine it could produce. There was a recently discharged veteran ready to buy every house built in the suburbs. Granddad told me of the joyous day when the Oldsmobile dealer called to say, "I have one new 1947 model coming in tomorrow. Do you want it?" By the early 1950s, however, wartime shortages were a thing of the past, supply was outstripping demand, and differentiated competitive alternatives were reaching the market. For many organizations, reliance on a production orientation was no longer viable.

In this section, I cited examples of organizations and sole proprietors operating under a production orientation. Let's now consider implications for an individual employee working for a business. I've noted that a production orientation is vulnerable to competitors who differentiate their offerings or who can produce the same thing for less. Those same vulnerabilities apply to individual employees and should serve as warning flags. An employee who performs a generic function may be replaced by an outsourcer who can do that function for less, perhaps half a world away. It is also possible that emerging technology will render their skills inadequate. Individuals operating under a production orientation need to assess their situation to determine its long-term viability. Ted Tinker, the clock repair guy, has a vital skill for which demand exceeds supply, with no competitive alternatives on the horizon, the only viable circumstances for a production orientation.

Form 2: Sales Orientation
Early in the decade of the 1950s, with the end of the post-World War II scarcities, many firms evolved toward a sales orientation. Their focus was still inward and upon themselves, but now their priority was figuring out how to get rid of what they did best and what they could most easily produce. The most simple solution was to organize a sales force and get Willy Loman (Arthur Miller: *Death of a Salesman*) out there to push products.

Faye may shift to a sales orientation when the gift shop has six bird feeders in inventory and won't take any more until they sell through. So, she organizes a sales force, her grandchildren, to scour the neighborhood in search of qualified buyers:

> BAM ! BAM ! BAM !
> "Whadaya want ?"
> "Hey, mister, ya wanna buy a bird feeder?"

There is an inevitable negative consequence of establishing a sales force: expenses increase, squeezing profits. The grandkids expect to get paid for working, and with a lot more than an extra stocking stuffer at Christmas. Additionally, there will be costs of employee benefits: Faye will have to provide milk and cookies for the sales force at the end of the day. Furthermore, with supply exceeding demand, she will be forced to initiate sales promotion activities, further depleting her margins:

> "We've got an Easter special: $5 off on every bird
>   feeder.
> "If you buy today I'll throw in a pound of birdseed,
>   absolutely free."

For an individual employee in a company, a sales orientation is tantamount to a reverse auction, and the worst of all possible worlds. In effect, the employee is trying to underbid all competitors. There was an example of this recently in a company that discovered it could outsource $200,000-a-year high tech functions to a third-world country for $60,000. They told employees to choose between a 70% pay cut, to $60,000, or termination. Many employees, seeing no alternative, took the pay cut. For those persons who chose to leave, their jobs were quickly filled by new hires anxious to get what they could get. This example should serve as fair warning to any person with a less-than-optimum production orientation. If you fail to take action, you might soon be forced into a sales orientation and a reduced income.

Form 3: Marketing Orientation

The profession of marketing as we know it today began to take shape in the late 1960s. By then, organizations had realized that a production or sales orientation was inappropriate for achieving long-term profit growth and that a different perspective was needed. The new paradigm that emerged, a radical change of thinking, was the marketing concept and the adaptation of a marketing orientation. Instead of looking inward upon itself and what it can do best, an organization with a marketing orientation looks outward toward customers and prospects. The essence of the marketing concept is to determine what constitutes value and benefits in the eyes of customers. An organization with a marketing orientation markets its products and services from the perspective of satisfying customer wants and needs, very different from a production or sales orientation, in which the objective is to unload production. Marketing professionals recognize this as the difference between features: facts about the product—company, service, system, etc.—and benefits—what those features mean to the customer. Customers don't want deadbolt locks, they want security. People don't want bouquets of flowers, they want love. Marketing professionals also know that customer-focused benefits may be satisfied with numerous product and service alternatives.

A firm with a marketing orientation will implement it with either, or both, of two approaches. The first approach would be to identify the many possible benefits of their product or service and then market to different prospects by focusing on benefits most important to them. Thus Faye would find both those who wanted a thoughtful gift to express affection and those who needed something to highlight their yard, and, for all, a bird feeder would be perfect. Fred Finagler, the insurance rep down the street, uses that approach. Whether you want to protect your loved ones, be secure in your golden years, or provide for a smooth succession in a business partnership, he has just the thing to satisfy your needs and everyone's, that's insurance. Same product, but, as he points out, different benefits that are important to different prospects.

The alternative and more sophisticated approach to implementing a marketing orientation is to first identify a promising target market and then develop, from the ground up, products and services specifically designed to address their wants and needs. Firms embarking on a marketing orientation might initially implement the first approach, identifying the numerous benefits of their current lines of products and services and communicating those benefits to customers and prospects. Next, they would employ the alternative approach in the process of new product development. As this process unfolds, the organization will discover that certain segments of the market offer greater profit potential than others. Under a production or sales orientation, the firm would target any and all prospective buyers. Now, in an evolving marketing perspective, they will begin to identify target market segments with higher potential and focus efforts accordingly.

It is important not to take a narrow view of what constitutes value in the eyes of a customer. Kraft Foods is known for their quality products, but channel members also like dealing with them because they act as partners in managing product presentation at outlet level and make it easy to do business with them in crediting and invoicing. On a personal level, I like shopping at Wal-Mart because of product selection and prices, but their associates also contribute value to my shopping experience. If I need help a knowledgeable associate will not only tell me what I need to know but will lead me where I need to go.

It is essential that individual employees adopt a marketing orientation. With a production orientation employees focus on the function they perform. If forced into a sales orientation they focus on performing that function more cheaply than competitive alternatives. But with a marketing orientation they look outward to assess what constitutes value to their employers. Then they determine what skills they need to learn, how to work and communicate effectively with colleagues, and ways in which they can demonstrate, objectively and measurably, contribution to the organization's profits. As a guideline, to be viable employees must demonstrate profit contribution of twice their salary. So if an individual is earning $100,000 a year he, or she, must account for combination of $200,000 increased profits, reduced costs, or expenses that would have been incurred had their accomplishments been outsourced. Then, that employee must document those achievements and communicate them to management. Back in my early days in the Fortune 500 I was earning $850 a month, decent for the late 1960s. After less than ten months with the company, I was able to reduce outside supplier costs by over $30,000. I documented this in a memo to my boss and followed up to be sure the achievement had been communicated to his boss. Shortly thereafter several persons in my department were laid off but I was rewarded with a nice raise. I have never doubted that my personal marketing program influenced career progress at that moment and forward. Management appreciates employees who understand the organization's bottom-line objectives and who demonstrate a contribution to the achievement of those objectives. Link all your activities to profit, and communicate your achievements.

Form 4: Societal Marketing Orientation
Since the 1990s, most marketing-oriented organizations have evolved to consider the collective needs of society and the environment in ad-

dition to organizational objectives and management's personal interests. The reason is simple and pragmatic: Good employees won't work for an organization that has a detrimental impact on the external environment or for a manager who is unethical. Also, in an age of media and attorneys, it pays to act properly. Recent corporate scandals have demonstrated that organizations and managers who act improperly will be found out and will pay the price.

As her business expands, Faye may adopt a societal marketing orientation by packing bird feeders in 100% recycled materials and contributing a portion of her profits to support restoration of the regional bird sanctuary. She may also discover opportunities to market her products to environmentally-sensitive prospects:

> "What problems are you having?"
> "My lawn is infested with insects."
> "How have you tried to get rid of them?"
> "I've sprayed the yard but the only stuff that works
>   is highly toxic. The kids are pretty tough but
>   I'm worried about the dog."
> "I've got an idea. If you could attract birds to your
>   yard they'd eat a lot of those insects.
>   Let me show you our line of bird feeders. . . ."

For a personal marketing plan, individuals can also adopt a societal marketing orientation involving themselves in activities that enhance the community. Such a focus will not contribute directly to their organization's bottom line but individuals may discover that their managers are impressed by a person who looks beyond his or her immediate self-interest.

CHAPTER 2

Marketing and the Organization

Everything in the organization revolves around marketing. Everything! Marketing conceptualizes and develops the firm's product/ service offerings and, through its sales and customer service arms, facilitates exchanges that enable the organization to achieve its objectives. All other functions and activities exist to support marketing, the source of revenue and profits. In this chapter I'll first discuss managing marketing and its ancillary systems. Then I'll address strategic alliances and partnerships in dealing with customers.

Defining Your Business

Just imagine yourself as a high-paid marketing expert, holding your initial meeting with top management of a large, prestigious client. After all the introductions and small talk you open with the question, "What business are you in?" What kind of reaction do you think you'd get? At first blush you might believe such a question would demonstrate a fundamental ignorance of the client's business and make you look like a fool who'd failed to do the most basic research and homework. But that question is precisely where marketing management must begin.

Over forty years ago Theodore Levitt highlighted the need to define business from a customer perspective instead of a production orientation ("Marketing Myopia," *Harvard Business Review*, July / August 1960.) He described numerous industries whose growth had slowed or stopped because management had described its business in terms of its current functions instead of customer needs. Levitt cited

11

the railroads as assuming themselves to be in the railroad business rather than the transportation business, causing them to be surpassed by competitive alternatives: cars, trucks, airplanes, and even telephones. He criticized the Hollywood studios for thinking they were in the movie business when they were actually in the entertainment business. It is interesting to note that the studios heeded Levitt's advice and have diversified and prospered in recent years. In a similar vein, the Atlanta Braves realize that although their major competition on the field may be the Marlins and the Phillies, their marketplace competitors are Six Flags and Pensacola Beach. After all, the Braves are not in the baseball business but in the wholesome family entertainment business. It's interesting to note that decades after Levitt wrote "Marketing Myopia," numerous organizations and industries continued to operate under a narrow, functional business definition. In the mid-1980s I was speaking with an executive from an American automobile manufacturer who described his firm as in "the new car business." This vulnerability was exploited by foreign nameplates who realized that customer satisfaction begins *after* the sale and defined themselves as being in "the personal transportation business." Fortunately for the American automobile companies they finally got it right by starting with quality products and building long-term customer relationships. On the flip side of that coin, producers of a leading encyclopedia kept insisting they were in the book publishing business despite the fact that their primary users—kids—wanted someone who was in the information-providing business and who had it on CD-ROM instead of in bulky, heavy books. Smith-Corona discovered too late that they were in the word and data processing business, not the typewriter business. Bye-bye. The jury is still out on Kodak, which once dominated the film market but has realized there no longer *is* a film business. It's the picture business.

Defining your business from the perspective of benefits customers seek, instead of a narrow description of products you produce, is the first step in moving away from a production orientation and embracing the marketing concept. That done, move on to the next step: differentiating yourself from the competition. What is it that makes your offerings different and better, providing unique value your target market will pay for?

Differentiating Products and Services

It is absolutely essential to differentiate your products and services from the competition or you will be forced to adopt a production/sales orientation, competing on price. A quarter-century ago Theodore Levitt said, "There is no such thing as a commodity. All goods and services can be differentiated and usually are." ("Marketing Success Through Differentiation—of Anything," *Harvard Business Review,* January/February 1980.) I would expand on Dr. Levitt's statement to say that if you believe your product or service is a commodity and cannot be differentiated, what it really means is that you are an inept marketer.

Products can be differentiated with features or convenient packaging which represents value to the target market. Services can be differentiated with tangible symbols and the professionalism of its sales representatives. And the organization can differentiate itself through advertising, promotion, and its management of customer relationships.

When selecting points of differentiation, be aware of the cost of adding a benefit as contrasted to its perceived value to the target market. Also, although you will not *rely* on costs of production to differentiate your products and services, it is consistent with a marketing orientation to *consider* them in differentiating. For example, if you enjoy a competitive advantage in materials and packaging costs for a particular product line, you might want to emphasize that line in head-to-head competition. Similarly, if you can more effectively execute a certain distribution strategy, consider making it a cornerstone of your overall marketing plan. In any case, evaluate *all* your points of differentiation and build your strategy up from there. Do *not* initially develop a grand strategy in the ivory tower and try to figure out the implementation. An excellent book on building strategy from the ground up is Al Ries and Jack Trout (1989), *Bottom-up Marketing,* New York: McGraw-Hill.

Differentiation and Specialization in The Organization

All good marketers differentiate their products and services to make them unique and special, creating value for the target market. Effective marketing managers apply the same principles of differentiation and specialization to their internal operations.

Specialization of labor is a concept that dates back to the earliest days of the industrial revolution. Its basic premise is simple: if every person performs the function at which he or she has a competitive advantage, the overall macroeconomic result is optimum productivity and societal living conditions. You may recognize this as consistent with a production orientation—do the same thing cheaper—or a marketing orientation—do it better and create added value that justifies the incremental cost. Be aware of these same principles in running a business.

Consider purchasing decisions. If customers perceive an item to be an undifferentiated commodity, they buy on price. All brands of paper for the copy machine are the same, so who's cheapest? If one manufacturer has a paper mill fifty miles away, and their competitor is 500 miles away, the former has a competitive advantage and may be able to deliver the goods at a more favorable price.

On the other hand, customers will pay more for a specialist if value exceeds price. If there's a leaky faucet in your break room, you could ask someone on your staff to repair it. By the time they figure out what parts are needed, make three round-trips to the hardware store, and do the work, they will have killed six hours and incurred a cost of sixty cents. A plumbing specialist could have done the job in ten minutes, but at a cost of sixty dollars. Although you may resent the idea of paying sixty dollars for ten minutes' work, it's a good decision. Your employee gets more done in those six hours working at his or her specialization and, net-net, you get better value. The fundamental implication of the concept of specialization of labor is that everyone should stick to what they do best. Now, let's take those ideas and apply them to marketing management.

As you define what business you are in categorize yourself as a *marketer*, not just a *producer*, in a wide customer-focused market. Marketing is your essential specialty. You may or may not have a competitive advantage as a producer of the products you market. If you do enjoy a competitive advantage in the production function you should continue to manufacture your products internally. If not, outsource that function to a contract manufacturer.

When business people hear the term "outsource," they often associate it with the loss of high-tech and manufacturing jobs to third-world countries, the example I cited in Chapter 1. Let's now take a much wider view of outsourcing and see how it represents an opportunity rather than just a threat.

An analysis of your production function might reveal that a contract manufacturing specialist could perform that role more effectively than you, particularly if your facilities are in operation 60 hours a week and the specialist is running 24/7. You would not only save on labor costs but would require considerably less capital for plant and equipment. One alternative, perhaps the lowest price, might be halfway around the world where workers are paid less than a dollar an hour. However, a domestic specialist might be a better choice. Chances are they could provide faster delivery; perhaps their highly-skilled workforce could provide more functions and higher quality; they might have more convenient terms, invoicing, and crediting; and they might offer an opportunity for a strategic alliance and partnership through distribution channels and at outlet level: all of which would add up to value well worth the price. The domestic specialist, taking a marketing perspective, could parley such differential advantages to prevail against the low-price production-oriented third world competitor.

Whether you are a marketing manager considering a specialty outsourcer or a specialty outsourcer seeking a customer and partner, focus on ways to enhance specialization and generate value. Ultimately, both parties come out ahead.

Specialization and outsourcing also applies to services. Chances are your organization does not specialize in janitorial services, landscaping, tax preparation, accounting, payroll, or legal services. If that's the case, outsource those functions to a specialist instead of doing them in-house. On the other hand, if you are the specialist in one of those services, market the benefits of having your organization be the one to provide those services to everyone else. It's not feasible to outsource janitorial and landscaping services halfway around the world but we often hear of high-tech services being outsourced at considerable savings. The implication is that someone in India can do the exact same thing for a fraction of the price. When you hear that, remember Theodore Levitt's declaration that there's no such thing as a commodity. Almost daily, someone tells me of dealing with a customer service rep on a telephone 8000 miles away. That interaction, and the client's reaction, occasionally falls short of expectations. What an opportunity for a domestic specialist!

Assessing and Allocating Costs

Competent marketing managers are always focused on revenue enhancement and cost control, objectives to be addressed simultaneously, not separately. Costs are either directly related to generating revenue or are supportive of activities that do. To the greatest extent possible budgeted expenses should be assigned to the cost of goods sold for specific products. For example, costs of point-of-sale (POS) materials for Product A should be charged to the product marketing budget rather than a catch-all budget for POS. Similarly, entertainment of a buyer to promote Product B should be charged to the product budget and not an overall travel and entertainment budget.

The cost of staff services should be addressed in a similar manner. As an example, expenses for Information Technology (IT) should be allocated to specific departments and products. Likewise, allocate fixed costs that support revenue-generating activities.

Managing and Allocating Fixed Costs

Back in Economics 101, you learned that fixed costs are those expenses that do not change as output increases or decreases. Examples would include plant and equipment, office space, and executive salaries. However, by treating fixed costs as variable costs and allocating them to departments and products you may discover that many so-called fixed costs can be reduced or eliminated. Let's say an IT person earns a salary of $60,000 a year and there is a direct cost of $20 an hour, or $40,000 a year, for her equipment and data services. Cost for this employee appears to be $100,000 a year, or $50 an hour. However, she has a supervisor who oversees eight IT persons and earns $80,000. Allocate the cost of the supervisor to the individual employee and there is an additional $10,000 per IT person, which raises the total to $110,000. Now add 50% in variable costs to cover benefits and other expenses and another 50% for her share of fixed costs including office space, furniture, and maintenance. In total, that $60,000 employee really costs the organization more like $220,000 a year, or $110 an hour.

Next step: from now on every time a department or product manager wishes to utilize this employee charge their budget at a rate of $110 an hour. All of a sudden people will begin to ask whether these staff services will generate revenue or reduce other costs to justify the expense. Additionally, you now realize that a specialty outsourcer, who will handle the project as well or better for $90 an hour, is actually a better value. Furthermore, whether you outsource an expense or eliminate it entirely, you suddenly discover that some of those so-called fixed costs can be reduced or eliminated. You no longer need 20,000 square feet of office space but can get along with half that amount. Insurance and maintenance fall proportionally. Costs of doing business drop and profits increase.

Managing Selling Expenses as Direct Costs

Generally, it is fairly routine to allocate direct costs of goods sold for manufactured products. I just noted the need to allocate internal expenses and charge them as direct costs. Now take this concept one step further by managing selling expenses as direct costs. To the greatest extent possible eliminate expense accounts entirely.

Let's say you paid the sales force $1,000,000 in commissions last year and incurred $250,000 in expense account reimbursements. Restructure the compensation system to increase commissions by 20% and let sales reps spend money as though it were their own, which it now really is. Commissions are increased to $1,200,000, expenses accounts have been eliminated, and you just added $50,000 to the bottom line. Now when reps stay in a $40 motel instead of a $100 luxury suite it's their own money they're saving. When they spend $80 entertaining a prospect there's likely a good return on investment. You're free of one more administrative hassle and may be in a position to eliminate a few more so-called fixed costs in bookkeeping and administration.

Employee Perspective

An individual employee must differentiate himself or herself just as the organization must differentiate its product offerings. You must find a way to provide superior value worth paying for in some distinct area of specialization directly related to revenue enhancement or cost control. Your contribution should be in some way unique—no one else can do what you do as well as you do it—and measurable by objective standards.

Remember Levitt's points about differentiation in the manner an entity conducts business. There's a lot to be said for being a person people like to be around and do business with. I hate meetings but when I have to be in one I assume the role of a facilitator, helping others to clarify their interests and finding ways for all participants to identify common ground and reach agreement. Colleagues have told me I'd helped them get more done in less time. I get to the office early and usually remain past designated office hours. In 17 years, I have never been late to class. All these little things add up to a perception of professionalism, essential to a personal marketing plan.

As you develop a unique area of specialization, it's possible you'll begin to consider the possibility of going into business for yourself as a specialty outsourcer instead of an employee. And generally, such opportunities will be more feasible if you are selling your professional expertise rather than a physical product. As you define and create your specialty, ask yourself whether there are other individuals and organizations who could utilize that specialty but only need it a few hours a week or a couple of weeks a year. If that's affirmative you may be defining a customer-oriented business to pursue.

In my latter days with the Fortune 500 I was developing and conducting sales and management training programs for a large corporation. Soon I realized that many smaller organizations could benefit from similar programs from a specialty outsourcer: Me! I took the plunge, went into business for myself, and never looked back. You won't, either.

Distinguishing Between Customers and Consumers

Marketing managers know that if they intend to be in business a few years from now customer service is a given, as essential to doing business as the product itself. Much has been written recently about the value of lifetime customers and how it is far more expensive to attract new customers than to nurture and retain your current base. Carl Sewell, a Cadillac dealer in Dallas, estimates the gross sales value of a lifetime customer is $517,000 (Sewell, Carl [2002], *Customers for Life.* New York: Currency Books). His book is a must-read for managers committed to excellent customer service. A couple of weeks ago I was chatting with the manager of the Wal-Mart just down the road. He astonished me with his estimate that the value of a lifetime household customer was $100,000: $2500 a year for forty years. That's why, he told me, they make a special point of treating customers right.

On a personal note, for over twenty years I was loyal to a national motel chain that promised the basic accommodations I wanted at a reasonable price. I visited one of their facilities about fifteen times a year and was generally satisfied until I had a totally unsatisfactory experience six months ago. On check-out I asked to speak to the manager but no management persons were on the premises. A housekeeper was tending the front desk and she was authorized only to take back the keys. Returning home the next day, I e-mailed their customer service department, described the situation, and stated I believed I was entitled to a refund. An hour later I received a computer-generated form letter, but nothing more. I sent off another e-mail, respectfully requesting that a human contact me. Someone responded with a personal e-mail saying she would look into the matter, but the next day I received a second computer-generated form letter that thanked me for my feedback, then stated that the matter was closed. Of course, I'll never do business with this chain again.

Who is Your Customer?

Competent marketing organizations, committed to excellent customer service, may fall short by failing to distinguish between customers and consumers. I'll address this point by first describing situations in which this issue is *not* a problem.

With services, the customer and the consumer are one and the same, since services cannot be warehoused and stored, and are simultaneously produced and consumed. Similarly, if you market business products such as raw materials, processed materials, or component parts, which are used by your partners to manufacture consumer products, it is clearly apparent that your customers are those business partners, not the ultimate consumer.

The customer and the consumer are also one and the same in a direct marketing business model, which does not utilize channel intermediaries. However, if you market physical products through traditional channels, those channel members—brokers, distributors, wholesalers, and retailers—are your customers. The next player down the channel, including the ultimate consumer, are *their* customers, not yours. Keep this in mind as you address issues of customer service.

Organizations marketing through traditional channels may delude themselves into believing they are properly managing customer service with programs directed solely at the ultimate consumer. They may offer 100% guarantees of satisfaction, telephone-and-web-based consumer hot lines, and special consumer relationship-building activities. Their promotions may feature coupons, rebates, contests, and sweepstakes designed to reward loyal consumers and build brand loyalty. But that only gets them halfway there, akin to driving from San Francisco to New York with a map that only goes as far as Des Moines.

Theodore Levitt's article on differentiation described methods by which an organization could differentiate itself by the manner in which it manages marketing and makes it easy to do business. In the quarter century since then, his ideas have been expanded upon to describe the concepts of partnerships and strategic alliances, all of which are predicated on a simple principle: A marketing-oriented firm operating through traditional channels strives to find ways to help its partners serve *their* customers. *That's* what it takes to get you from Des Moines to New York.

Follow the Money!
I've described the importance of defining your customers—whoever's name is on the check—and distinguishing them from the ultimate consumer. Let's look at an innovative marketing program that followed the money to identify a customer seldom targeted in its industry.

One of my colleagues is the marketing manager for a major medical products firm. Traditionally, their representatives have concentrated their selling efforts on physicians, surgeons, and health care providers, persons utilizing the firm's products in surgical procedures. He built a strategy upon a different approach, recognizing that the money paying for everything was coming from insurance companies and large corporations with internally-funded medical benefits programs. In essence, physicians, surgeons, and health care providers were channel intermediaries serving the ultimate consumer, the patient. His first step was to meet with management from the insurance companies and large corporations to determine their current costs for procedures utilizing the line of products his company produced. To keep the numbers simple let's say the average cost of the medical products was $2000 and fees for physicians and hospitalization were $8000, for a total cost of $10,000. He confirmed that those insurance companies and corporations, as expected, were receptive to the prospect of providing a comparable quality of care at a lower cost.

He next approached the leading physicians and hospitals to determine how many procedures they were doing for the fee of $8000 each. Again, to keep it simple, let's say it was one a week. Then, he asked whether they would be willing to reduce their fee to $6000 if they could do one a *day*, using his firm's products in the procedure. They were very interested, predictable because of their production orientation.

Finally, he returned to the insurance companies and corporations to consummate details of this complex strategic alliance in which, thanks to the higher volume being generated, he was able to reduce his product cost to $1500. Net-net: cost for the insurance companies was reduced, the physicians and hospital increased their earnings, and his company improved their total profits.

Whatever business you're in, if you operate through traditional channels, the entity that is the source of your revenue is your customer. Help them and everyone down the line to serve *their* customers, all the way down to the ultimate consumer. With strategic alliances and partnerships everybody wins.

CHAPTER 3

The External Environment

In the last chapter I described the role of marketing in the organization and points concerning effective marketing management. Now let's turn our sights to the world outside the organization, the external marketing environment. Some of these factors are uncontrollable although marketing managers must be apprised of them and act to address challenges and opportunities they present. Other factors may be impacted to a limited degree. Finally, certain factors are in direct play with your organization. Let's look at all these external factors beginning with the uncontrollable.

Uncontrollable External Factors

Demographics

The most important uncontrollable external factor is demographics, the statistical measurement of observable characteristics such as age, race, ethnic background, household composition, and location. Many long-term demographic trends have dramatically altered the marketing landscape.

Thanks largely to the aging of the baby boomers, those persons born between 1946 and 1964, the median age of Americans is increasing. As the boomers mature more and more of them will become empty nesters, two-person households with children living independently. These couples, at their peak earning years, will have more discretionary income for entertainment and travel. As years go by they will require more medical treatment. Many will elect to leave their traditional residences in favor of active retirement communities. Steadily, fewer will be wage earners and more will be net consumers of products and services. This will have the positive implication of providing jobs for those individuals and organizations that produce those products and services.

America is becoming more racially and ethnically diverse. This is especially notable due to immigration of Asians on the west coast and Hispanics in the south and southwest. The population of African-Americans is increasing as well, particularly in metro areas. These trends have implications for the products and services these persons will need and also for the impact they will make on labor markets. New immigrant families may require schools and social services, straining resources at the local level.

No longer is the term "household" synonymous with a unit composed of mom, dad, and the kids. Marketing managers need to consider the implications of single parents with children and affluent young professionals who delay marriage and children. We cannot ignore the increasing visibility of same-sex households and the opportunities they present in the development and positioning of products and services.

Generally, population has shifted toward the west, southwest, and south, to a large degree a reflection of immigration. However, there have been some very interesting shifts within metro areas. Starting in the 1940s and 1950s large numbers of persons fled to the suburbs, abandoning core cities to poverty and decay. Recently, however, many of these cities have enjoyed a renaissance, with neighborhoods being restored and property values rising, thanks largely to the influx of young professionals. Many of these people, in a complete reversal of past trends, live in the city and work in the suburbs. As a personal observation, I've noted that the worst rush hour traffic from the north side of Chicago is now getting out of the city in the morning and going into the city at night. Effective marketing managers are alert to changes like these, always thinking about what opportunities they might present.

The Economy and the World Political Scene
Depending on what you market, your sales may be dramatically affected, slightly affected, or not fazed in the least by the overall economy and events taking place on the world political scene. If you market cosmetics or cigarettes, you might as well skip this segment entirely as your sales will be essentially unaffected by recession or

world events. However, most business will be impacted to some degree and should have contingency plans for various scenarios.

Big-ticket items, particularly housing and autos, will be affected by changes in interest rates. Rising rates increase monthly payments, disqualifying some prospects and forcing others to settle for something at a lower gross sales price. In the housing market a continued rise in rates may so reduce the buyer pool that gross prices drop, causing a ripple effect throughout the housing industry and for its product and service providers.

A downturn in the economy will have a minimal effect on staples but might have a very significant impact on discretionary expenditures, items whose purchase can be postponed or eliminated. Generally, recessions have the greatest effect on working-class people. Business may drop at the local amusement park, but there's no slowdown for $500-a-day luxury cruises.

For your business or yourself personally it would be prudent to contemplate potential geopolitical events. What would happen if the price of gasoline hit $5 a gallon? Or $8 a gallon? What would be the implication, especially in the northeast, of oil going to $80 a barrel? How about $100 a barrel? It is conceivable that events could occur to precipitate such a spike in prices. Geopolitical or domestic events could cause a similar jump in the price of electricity as was demonstrated in the California power crisis a few years back. Think about what such energy prices would do to you and whether you can take steps in advance.

It isn't possible to predict specific future terrorist attacks but it would be wise to consider the implications of an international atmosphere in which Americans would be reluctant to visit a large number of other nations in the world. Similarly, what would it mean if an increasing number of people elected to remain in their homes and go out only at certain times and to certain places?

It's not pleasant to think about disruptive events but it is no longer reasonable to stick your head in the sand and refuse to acknowledge them. That's why you carry insurance, isn't it?

Technology
I list technology as the last uncontrollable factor because technology is the business for many firms and with it they affect the economy and

society every day. For other organizations, innovative adaptations of technology have dramatically impacted how companies and entire industries serve their customers.

A detailed description of technology and its applications goes far beyond the scope of this book, so I'll limit my comments to a few basics. First and foremost you must fully adopt technology for your people to be their most productive and to make it easy for all your customers to do business with you. Beyond that, consider the implications of technology when developing a marketing strategy.

I've described the need to differentiate your product offerings and to specialize with some competitive advantage. As long as you maintain that differentiation and specialization you can command a premium price by creating value customers are willing to pay for. A question you must answer, then, is whether technology has the potential to affect competition's ability to neutralize that differential advantage, and in what time frame. Internet-oriented businesses have discovered that competitive firms can be up and running in a matter of days. More traditional organizations have discovered that special fares and promotions communicated on their websites were matched by the competition within hours. And all types of organizations have discovered that their unique technology innovations were quickly thrust into the public domain. Secrets and unique competitive advantage are fleeting in cyberspace. The lesson seems clear: Stay on the cutting edge of technology and take advantage of it in every way possible, but don't rely on it to keep you ahead of the pack for long.

Impactable External Factors

Social Change

Many marketing experts classify social change as an uncontrollable external factor, implying that individuals and organizations are being carried by the currents of a river. Extending that analogy, these experts advise you to tap into the power of the flow and be aware of the potential flood that might sweep you away. I don't entirely agree with that perspective.

Certainly we must recognize societal changes and assess their potential impact on individuals and organizations. However, those changes are not reflections of the inevitable course of history, a river exempt from influence and control. Societal changes do not just happen: they are caused to happen. Specific individuals and organizations *make* them happen. A more appropriate analogy would be motors that drive social change. Seeing yourself as a motor driving change, rather than floating down a river, is an essential step to embracing a proactive marketing strategy.

A starting point for affecting social change is establishing ethical standards. Recent scandals in a wide variety of organizations attest to a need to address personal and professional conduct. Ask yourself if your standards reflect expediency and a tacit acceptance of unethical conduct because "everybody else does it" and your objective is short-term survival in a dog-eat-dog world. To use another analogy, have you elected to light a single candle rather than curse the darkness? If you believe that good employees would want to work for a company—and good prospects would want to do business with a company—that manages its affairs ethically and acts respectfully toward every individual, it is in your long-term best interest to adopt such standards. The beacon of light is built one small candle at a time.

Some organizations, generally not-for-profit special interest groups, exist for the primary purpose of driving or restraining social change. Though they primarily market ideas rather than products or services, they employ the same marketing strategies and tactics as organizations selling soap or life insurance. Select any controversial social agenda and you're likely to find groups on opposing ends of the issue attempting to drive social change by winning the hearts and minds of their target market, pressuring lawmakers at every level.

The world's largest organization, the Roman Catholic Church, certainly did not haphazardly choose a Polish Cardinal to become Pope in 1978. Recognizing the threat, and vulnerability, of the atheistic Soviet Union, they reached out to the Polish people and the emerging resistance movement in the Gdansk shipyards. Their situation analysis determined that the people of Poland would stand up and, if necessary, give their lives for their faith. It was the beginning of the end for Soviet domination in Eastern Europe, leading, inevitably, to the fall of the Soviet Union itself.

Traditional product and service organizations also act as visible motors of social change. The civil rights movement was afforded national visibility when the Brooklyn Dodgers brought Jackie Robinson to the major leagues in 1947. Later, forward-looking organizations began featuring African-Americans in commercial messages, promoting the image of minorities as mainstream citizens. Those early actions helped build the climate of respect for diversity that continues to this day. Today, numerous organizations identify themselves with a wide range of issues and causes through product positioning, advertising, and with their product assortment and standards. Whether it be environmental sensitivity or addressing the exploitation of child labor, organizations drive social change in a manner consistent with attracting and retaining customers.

Individuals also are motors of social change, particularly if afforded the power of affiliation with an organization. Leaders of not-for-profit organizations are often synonymous with the message and social objectives of the organization. High-profile executives such as Bill Gates of Microsoft may direct personal and organizational resources toward activities and programs that enhance social change. Additionally, many opinion leaders, particularly those who have attained visibility through sports or other entertainment fields, may affiliate with organizations as a spokesperson for their products while simultaneously partnering in the promotion of social changes.

Organizations and influential individuals are the motors of social change. Long-term marketing strategy must address whether and how to proactively drive change, or choose to monitor and react to those changes as they occur.

Fads and Crazes
Whereas social changes are generally long-term, fads and crazes can pop up overnight. Some are cute or at least harmless, like pet rocks and the Macarena. Others, such as the low-carb craze, were a rude kick in the shins for many organizations. For the beer companies, the low-carb craze was amusing, as everyone brought out new products and repositioned existing brands, but just as with cigarettes and cosmetics, total market sales were unaffected. Not so for firms manufacturing, or restaurants featuring, pasta products, some of whom endured downturns in sales or worse. On a personal note, I'd been paying $1.25 for

a box of my favorite shells and white cheddar. All of a sudden, it was on a permanent sale price of 99¢, compounded with a 50¢-off coupon in the Sunday paper. My in-home inventory peaked at a three-year supply, assuming I eat it at least once a day. Yes, I helped them maintain their pre-craze sales level, but at a net of 49¢ a box, I don't believe their margins were any too hefty.

Just as with social change, fads and crazes don't just happen. Someone causes them, though in the low-carb craze it was a diet book rather than an organization's proactive strategy. Perhaps you'll be fortunate enough at some point to set a craze in motion, pushing all the right buttons to have the world clamoring for your products and decrying all the competitive alternatives. But don't bet on it. Better to stay tuned to the world, quickly recognize when a fad or craze is for real, and act. If you can position your product or service to complement the craze, be the first in your category to do so and take the leadership position. If not, if you're pasta in low-carb land, think of it as a terrorist attack, batten down the hatches, and ride out the storm as best you can, if you can.

The Regulatory Environment

This is not a book about business law, and for any question concerning legal issues, consult your attorney. However, in this segment I will briefly note major regulatory agencies and in the final chapter some basics about legal points in setting prices.

If you manufacture consumer products used in and around the home familiarize yourself with the Consumer Product Safety Commission (CPSC) which has the power to establish mandatory standards to protect the consumer's safety and health. The CPSC has the authority to ban the sale of unsafe products and, if necessary, to fine and jail offending organizations and their officers.

Attempting to establish a monopoly or a trust, acting in restraint of trade, and engaging in unfair competitive practices may put you in violation of the Sherman Anti-trust Act (1890) and/or bring you under the jurisdiction of the Federal Trade Commission (FTC). The FTC is also empowered to take action against any firm deemed to have engaged in deceptive advertising. Agreements between the FTC and offending firms may take the form of a consent decree—the firm agrees to stop doing what the FTC considered improper—or a requirement that the offending firm conduct corrective advertising to counteract misleading advertising of the past. Corrective advertising is easy to miss, and the objective of firms running it is that customers are totally oblivious to the confession of past sins. Copy does not read, "Hey, we shouldn't have told you that this pill will make you lose fifty pounds of ugly fat in sixty days. If you keep eating all the same stuff and spend all evening on the couch you'll be lucky to lose two pounds." No, they'll have some young beauty bound out of the surf, jog a few yards up to the camera, and say something like, "Of course, Fat-a-way is just one part of a total program of diet and fitness. Start today!"

Legal and regulatory issues, too, are often classified as uncontrollable external factors. However, they are often impactable, at least to a certain degree. Issues of product safety and deceptive advertising may be open to interpretation and negotiation. A cease-and-desist order from the FTC may be challenged in court. And, similar to social change, individuals and organizations may affect the direction and scope of the law. Should you wish to verify that, do a head count of the lobbyists in Washington and your State House.

The Competitive Environment

There's one element of the external environment you deal with every day, and that's the competition. Consistent with the perspective of a marketing orientation let's think of the "competition" as any alternative to the products and services you market. So, if you manage an upscale beach resort, the competition includes a resort in the mountains, a cruise to Alaska, or pay-per-view movies on Cable TV. No effective marketing manager develops a strategic plan or devises short-term tactics in a vacuum. You must always consider the competitive environment.

To illustrate this point, let's consider some of my shameless sports analogies. When preparing for the Super Bowl teams develop their game plan based on the competitive situation as much as on their own strengths. If the enemy is perceived to be weak in pass defense in the secondary, go at them with long passes. If they've had to use substitutes on the front line, go straight at them with a ground game right up the middle. Similarly, in marketing, go beyond your own points of differentiation and competitive advantages to seek out vulnerabilities that can be exploited.

Sports and marketing are both games of adjustments, play by play, day by day. As you prepare the game plan put yourself in the competitor's shoes and ask: If I do this, what are they likely to do in response to it? How long will it take them to respond and how effective will that response be? So, if on your first offensive series you burn them with an 80-yard touchdown pass you would expect them to respond with some defensive changes. If those changes are effective in stopping your long passing game you'll have to try a different tack. On the other hand, if you burn them three times before they figure out what to do, it's 21–0 in the first quarter and the ultimate outcome no longer in doubt.

Baseball is a game of adjustments at-bat by at-bat. Good pitchers keep a running tally on every batter in the league. If a batter gets a home run off a good pitcher, that batter is unlikely to see the same pitch again. Conversely, if a batter swings weakly at a particular pitch he'll keep seeing it until he learns how to hit it or to take it without swinging. I remember opening day for the Cubs a few years back when a rookie outfielder made his major league debut hitting an astonishing four home runs. Suddenly, all of Chicago was touting him as a cinch for Rookie of the Year and the All-Star team. Until the next day, that is, when the opposing team discovered he just couldn't lay off a curve ball out of the strike zone. He never could hit one, but neither could he just let it go. He was out of baseball soon thereafter.

The competition is not going to sit back and let you play your game. In fact, they'll do everything within their power to force you to play *their* game. Reactive managers respond to competition's actions. Proactive managers anticipate those actions and have already formulated a counterstrike.

Strategic Perspectives

It makes no sense to go head-to-head against an established competitor unless you have some differential advantage, since you'll be forced to wage the war with a lower price. Undercutting the big guys on price is generally not a viable option as they're likely to prevail in a battle of attrition unless, as noted, you have a favorable cost structure and can profit with a production orientation. As a rule you need to be "something they ain't," providing some special value they don't offer to some special target market they don't adequately serve.

Implicit in the terms "some special value" and "some special target market" is the perspective of thinking small. More opportunities for *profitable* products and services may be found in niche markets where a narrow target market will pay a premium to get benefits uniquely valuable to them. Let everyone else fight it out digging through the hills in search of the ever-elusive mother lode while you walk serenely through the stream picking up the individual nuggets.

Be Your Own Toughest Competitor
I've worked with several organizations who "enjoyed" a position of market share dominance in their product category. I put "enjoyed" in quotation marks because these firms found themselves in a continuous battle to defend their turf, dealing with a never-ending series of competitive onslaughts nipping at their heels. Playing defense is reactive in nature, and those experiences convinced me it's more effective, and more fun, to be the nipp*er* instead of the nipp*ee.* Instead of permitting someone else to drive you crazy, be your own toughest competitor.

This perspective flies in the face of conventional business thinking. An executive of a leading rental car company, whose counters were all in the expensive airport locations, rejected the idea of establishing a competitive company doing business in the much cheaper locations peripheral to the airport. To paraphrase his colorful language, he linked the proposal to "watering down the soup." However, recent start-ups of low-fare carriers by traditional carriers within the airline industry have embraced the concept of being their own toughest competitor instead of reactively defending their turf.

If an organization is going to compete with itself, management must decide whether the competing business unit is going to be *real* competition or just another entry in a competitive segment. An example of the latter alternative was the introduction of small cars—the Corvair, Falcon, and Valiant—by the American automobile companies in 1960, in response to the competitive onslaught of foreign compact cars, particularly the Volkswagen. The American companies wanted models to compete against VW, but never intended those entries to be viable competition against their high-profit gas guzzlers. Consequently, the door was left open for the Japanese invasion, particularly by Honda, Toyota, and Datsun (now Nissan). Whereas VW had made a dent in the traditional gas-guzzler segment, the Japanese carved out a gaping hole. In retrospect, had the American companies attacked themselves with high-quality compact cars in 1960, the intensity of the Japanese invasion might have been far less disruptive.

It will be interesting to see how things play out in the airline industry. If, and it's a very big and uncertain if, the traditional business model is going the way of the leisure suit, the optimum strategy for their parent companies may be to have their low-fare business units attack the entire traditional carrier segment, including themselves. Let their traditional business units, and competition's traditional business units, adjust to the changing marketplace and survive or perish according to their abilities. Their flagship brand may go into Chapter 11, but the low-fare business unit may become a leader in the emerging segment. The alternative may be that their flagship brand still goes into Chapter 11 but the low-fare business unit is an also-ran.

Shift the Market

Over the years, I've dealt with dozens of organizations fighting the battle for market share. Generally, they have an entry in several product categories and fight it out for market share within each category. Then they add up the share points within each category to get a grand total share for the overall product class. A while back, however, I ran across an organization that adopted an innovative approach that might work for others: instead of battling for market share within each category, shift the market itself. Here's an example of how this can work.

Often, your competitor has a relatively strong share position in a certain product category but may, and this is essential, have a lesser position in other categories. To keep this simple, let's consider a market of two competitors each featuring two products.

In this market hamburgers have 80% total market share and chicken sandwiches 20%. There are two competitors, each of whom sells both hamburgers and chicken sandwiches: Hamburger City, the dominant player, and Chicken Heaven, a distant number two. Overall, Hamburger City dominates the hamburger segment, accounting for 90% of all hamburger sales. Chicken Heaven sells the remaining 10%. By contrast, Chicken Heaven accounts for 70% of all chicken sandwiches sold. Thus, Hamburger City sells the remaining 30%.

To calculate market share for a total product class add up the share points within every product category. So, Hamburger City has a 90% share of the hamburger market, times the 80% importance of hamburgers in the total product class, yielding 72% of the class as hamburgers sold by Hamburger City. Likewise, Hamburger City has a 30% share of the chicken sandwich market, times the 20% importance of chicken sandwiches in the total product class, yielding 6% of the class as chicken sandwiches sold by Hamburger City. Total product class share for Hamburger City is 72% + 6%, or 78%.

Similarly, Chicken Heaven has a 10% share of the hamburger market, times the 80% importance of hamburgers in the total product class, yielding 8% of the class as hamburgers sold by Chicken Heaven. Likewise, Chicken Heaven has a 70% share of the chicken sandwich market, times the 20% importance of chicken sandwiches in the total product class, yielding 14% of the class as chicken sandwiches sold by Chicken Heaven. Total product class share for Chicken Heaven is 8% + 14%, or 22%.

These figures, for the base period, are summarized in Table 3-1.

Traditionally, a market follower like Chicken Heaven would see its greatest opportunity for improving market share as attacking the market leader in their dominant category. Thus, Chicken Heaven would go after the hamburger market dominated by Hamburger City. Simultaneously, they would attempt to maintain share leadership in their primary category, chicken sandwiches. An ambitious goal might be to increase their share of the hamburger market by a factor of one-fifth, from a 10% share to a 12% share. If successful, as summarized in Table 3-2, Chicken Heaven's product class share would increase from 22% to 23.6%, as product class share for Hamburger City declined to 76.4% from 78%.

An alternative strategy, which might be easier and less costly to implement, would be to shift the importance of the segments them-

TABLE 3-1
Market Shares—Base Period

	Hamburger City			Chicken Heaven		
	Category Importance	Share within Category	Product Class Share	Category Importance	Share within Category	Product Class Share
Hamburgers	80% X	90% =	72%	80% X	10% =	8%
Chicken Sandwiches	20% X	30% =	6%	20% X	70% =	14%
Total	100%		78%	100%		22%

TABLE 3-2
Market Shares—Hamburger Promo

	Hamburger City			Chicken Heaven		
	Category Importance	Share within Category	Product Class Share	Category Importance	Share within Category	Product Class Share
Hamburgers	80% X	88% =	70.4%	80% X	12% =	9.6%
Chicken Sandwiches	20% X	30% =	6%	20% X	70% =	14%
Total	100%		76.4%	100%		23.6%

selves rather than battle for market share within segments. In our example, if chicken sandwiches increase category importance from 20% to 25%, with hamburgers falling from 80% to 75%, as illustrated in Table 3-3, product class share for Chicken Heaven increases from 22% to 25%, as Hamburger City falls from 78% to 75%, despite the fact that shares within product categories remain unchanged.

The principle of this example can be applied to any competitive environment. Identify those segments in which you have relative strength and determine whether you can cause that segment to increase its overall importance. Likewise, reduce the importance of segments in which you are relatively weak.

The organization I worked with that took this innovative approach implemented it from the bottom up. They enjoyed relative strength in Product A whereas competition dominated Product B. Their strategy was to parlay a differential advantage in distribution and materials handling for Product A to encourage channel members to emphasize it in promotions and give it more visibility at outlet level. But however you execute such an approach, through distribution channels or by directly influencing the consumer, shifting the total market toward segments in which you enjoy relative strength will result in an overall gain in market share.

A Global Perspective

You might be tempted to skip over this final chapter segment if you only market products and services domestically believing you need not be concerned about a global perspective. But today everything is global and there's no such thing as an impregnable local business. If you don't believe me just ask someone formerly employed in the domestic textile or consumer electronics industries. No matter what your product or service, there may be a competitor half a world away anxious to relieve you of your livelihood.

The world is becoming a global marketplace, with trade barriers falling and the Internet facilitating communication and exchanges worldwide. Earlier, I noted that foreign competition has forced organizations and individuals to find new and innovative ways to create value the marketplace will pay for. Don't expect an organization to

Market Shares—Shift the Market

	Hamburger City			Chicken Heaven		
	Category Importance	Share within Category	Product Class Share	Category Importance	Share within Category	Product Class Share
Hamburgers	75% X	90% =	67.5%	75% X	10% =	7.5%
Chicken Sandwiches	25% X	30% =	7.5%	25% X	70% =	17.5%
Total	100%		75%	100%		25%

remain profitable or an individual to put bread on the table doing the same old job the same old way as only a few years ago.

The shift to globalization has been disruptive. Ross Perot predicted a "great sucking sound" of American blue-collar jobs going to Mexico upon implementation of the North American Free Trade Agreement (NAFTA) among the United States, Canada, and Mexico. More recently, some persons have advocated subsidizing higher-paid domestic workers or penalizing firms that outsource generic tasks and services to foreign firms. Over the long run, however, the global marketplace will reward organizations and individuals that provide the greatest value for the price. Conversely, individuals, organizations, and nations that attempt to subsidize inferior productivity or fail to provide comparable value for the price will fall into economic decline. All those things that made individuals, organizations, and nations great in the past will not ensure survival in the future. The global marketplace demands education, training, and value-creating skills as the prerequisites for survival.

Basic Considerations for Going Global
The first consideration in developing a global strategy is ensuring that your home turf is adequately defended against a foreign invasion. Not much point going out on a patrol to Sherwood Forest only to return and discover the castle has been overrun. That done, the major question is whether you can sell the exact same products worldwide, a global standardization approach. Levi 501s, the button-fly jeans, appeal to a worldwide audience, as do Timex watches. A Coca-Cola in Zurich should match the one you had in Albany. On the other hand, you might elect to feature different products and/or different messages in various markets. Hamburger City might need to diversify its product line in places where cows are revered. Likewise, they probably wouldn't have a significant demand for baby back ribs where pork is reviled.

You must consider the level of economic development in the target country. A nation with average annual household income of $100,000 might seem lucrative for marketing kitchen appliances until you learn that 1% of the households earn $10 million a year and the remaining 99% earn $10 a month and have no electricity. On the other hand, a takeoff economy like Viet Nam may present enough future potential to justify either direct investment or a joint venture with a local firm.

It is essential to have an appreciation for a nation's culture and their ways of doing business. Slapping people on the back, yelling "Yee-hah," and machine-gunning business cards around the room may be a great attention-getter in West Texas but will not play in Tokyo. In some nations it would be inappropriate and illegal to offer a bribe to government officials. Elsewhere, it's the only way to get the boat unloaded. The fact that it may be a violation of U.S. law for American firms to pay bribes in foreign countries is bound to make your day more interesting.

Be aware of potential problems with exchange control, difficulties in getting profits out of a foreign country. This was an issue in the old Soviet Union, where the ruble was a non-convertible currency. Pepsico had an interesting approach to this challenge, taking its profits in the form of Soviet vodka. Should you confront exchange control in a nation where you are considering doing business explore a similar opportunity for barter in a partnership with an organization in the target country.

If you are a relatively small firm it may not be practical to consider building manufacturing facilities, opening offices, or to generate the capital necessary for a joint venture or direct investment to create foreign subsidiaries in every target country. Under those circumstances, you might consider exporting or licensing.

Exporting is selling domestically-produced products to customers in another country. Almost certainly this would necessitate employing buyers and agents to attain and manage distribution through local channels. Earlier I noted outsourcing of manufacturing to contractors as an alternative to investing in production facilities, equipment, and personnel. Even if you insource production domestically, there may be advantages to contract manufacturing internationally. Production costs may be less, transportation costs reduced, and a manufacturing partnership in the target region may enhance prospects for other strategic alliances in channels of distribution and with firms providing ancillary services.

An alternative to manufacturing and exporting domestically or internationally is licensing: legally permitting another firm to use your trademarks, brand names, and processes. A second-tier brand of beer, in the popular price segment, wanted to enter the Canadian market but potential sales were too low to justify a direct investment. Exporting was not viable since distribution and transportation costs would have priced the brand too high to compete in its segment. Thus, the parent company entered into a licensing arrangement with a Canadian brewer that had an established production and distribution system. Similarly, an American operator of theme parks wanted to expand into Japan but was unfamiliar with the culture and lacked the necessary contacts and alliances. Rather than go it alone they established a licensing arrangement with a Japanese company to operate their theme park in Tokyo. Explicit in this understanding is that the license may be revoked and granted to another organization if the licensee does not properly present and manage the parent company's brands.

If you're wearing a T-shirt supporting your favorite university, sports team, or Hollywood character, it's likely the product of a licensing arrangement to use a name or symbol identified as a registered trademark. I own licensed T-shirts and polo shirts with the trademark "University of Georgia" or the trademarked form of the letter "G." Similarly, I have T-shirts that feature the letter "C" in a format which is the intellectual property of the Chicago Cubs. On the other hand I have another T-shirt, which I got at half the price, that simply says "Georgia," a term not protected by copyright and not requiring a licensing arrangement for its use.

Many service businesses and not-for-profit organizations want to take advantage of the value of their trademarks and symbols, but have no interest in diversifying into T-shirts, coffee mugs, and cake decorating. Licensing is a sensible option for them and a partnership opportunity for organizations whose main product line *is* T-shirts, coffee mugs, and cake decorating.

Chapter 4

The Decision-Making Process

In this chapter, I'll discuss the decision-making process, contrasting individual consumers and business-to-business (B2B) markets. Though steps of the process are similar, B2B marketing, including channel management of consumer products through the distribution chain, emphasizes one-on-one personal selling. By contrast, marketing to consumers, except through direct channels, is much more impersonal. In direct channels, the focus may range from being very personal, as in sales of insurance or financial services to individual clients, to being almost as impersonal as selling off-the-shelf products, as illustrated by inbound telemarketing through an "800" number. Psychology describes the decision-making processes of individuals, generally applicable to B2B communication, whereas consumer marketing assesses its target market as a totality in which we often cannot describe exactly what's going on with any one prospect.

Steps in Decision-Making

The decision-making process begins with physical and psychological drives that are addressed by cues designed to elicit a specific response —the exchange. Essential to successful marketing is an understanding of those drives and how they can be satisfied, points to be addressed in detail later in this chapter.

Need Recognition

The first step of the decision-making process is need recognition, an imbalance between where the individual is and where he or she would prefer to be. A simple example would be a physiological need about which the person is consciously aware: I'm hungry. Where am I going

41

to go for lunch? This basic need can be satisfied by a large number of alternatives, from a burger and fries at Hamburger City to the twenty-dollar luncheon buffet at the Gulf Breeze Gentleman's Club. Marketers know, however, that simple physiological needs do not command premium prices. Thus, if the *only* need addressed is hunger, the prospect will opt for Hamburger City or perhaps a peanut butter sandwich at home.

Far more lucrative are upper-level needs of respect, esteem, and personal fulfillment, about which the prospect may not be immediately or consciously aware. For instance, a prospect unconsciously feeling unwanted and unloved will find no satisfaction at Hamburger City, where the teen-aged staff will ignore him completely. On the other hand, the hostesses at the Gulf Breeze Gentleman's Club will indirectly assure him that he's intelligent, charming, and witty, commanding a far greater value.

Successful marketers address *existing* needs rather than attempt to create needs. For instance, if certain persons have no interest in being active and physically fit, it is futile to attempt to convince them they should feel differently than they do and that they need your product or service to change their lives. Successful marketers do not manipulate prospects with false promises, but permit them to evaluate alternatives in the free market. Prospects vote with their money and their feet. Repeat business and referrals are the scorecard by which you measure need satisfaction.

Information Search
Before making a purchasing decision prospects conduct some form of information search, although they are completely unconscious of this throughout the process. The extent of this search tends to reflect the perceived level of risk and complexity of the decision. Low involvement decisions for the purchase of low-risk, low-cost items frequently purchased will tend to be the least complex routine response behavior. Whenever you're low on gas you stop at the same station as usual and fill the tank. You walk in and grab a can of pop out of the cooler, displayed with pricing and point-of-sale. It's lunchtime, you're hungry, and without thinking you pull into the drive-through at Hamburger City for two triple cheeseburgers and large fries. Saturday after work,

you drop by Betty's Beer Barn and grab a 6-pack of the same brand of beer you've been buying for years. These actions require no contemplation, just action, solely confined to an internal information search. Nothing external to you influences the decision.

If we consider the hundreds of buying decisions we make each week and the thousands of messages to which we are exposed, it's a good thing for our sanity's sake that we aren't carefully contemplating our needs and consciously monitoring our information-search minute by minute. But our needs are constantly changing and evolving, and with them our openness and susceptibility to new information. What was once routine response behavior shifts to the next-highest level of complexity: limited decision-making, a fairly quick limited-consequence decision in which the prospect is likely to be influenced by advertising, promotion, and other external information sources.

We often associate limited decision-making with items of moderate cost, likely infrequently purchased, representing a fairly quick limited-consequence decision. Examples might include buying furniture, a refrigerator, or calling a plumber. Let's consider each of these situations.

Buying furniture is a classic illustration of limited decision-making. After several years, two kids, and a dog, Fred and Martha gradually reach need recognition that the sofa and chairs just ain't what they used to be. Fred's doing pretty well at the feed store, Martha just got a promotion at the bank, and they're beginning to want, and able to afford, some nicer and newer things. One evening, playing bridge with friends from church, they can't help but notice the new living room suite because the lady of the house points it out, tells them where she bought it, and brags about how much she paid for it. The next day Martha notices an ad for furniture in the Sunday paper and comments to Fred, "That's no big deal. They have their real sales in April and October."

Until that moment, Martha had never been aware of seeing the store's ad but does not pause to wonder how she could have been aware of their promotion schedule. Decision-making now begins in earnest at a level of conscious awareness. After some comparison shopping over a period of several months they find what they like and dream of inviting people to come over and play bridge at *their* place.

Let's consider the other end of the limited decision-making spectrum: calling a plumber. *No one* does an information search for a plumber. *No one* does advance planning to ascertain that Plumber A would be the best one to handle the flood caused by the hot water heater but Plumber B would be a better choice when the septic tank backs up into the downstairs bathtub. Disaster occurs and you head for the Yellow Pages, drawn to the full-color display ads that proclaim how many years in business, licensing and certification, and their areas of specialization. But then, and only then, do you recall that one of those Yellow Pages ads is for a plumber you've seen advertised on TV. You can't remember anything about the TV commercial, just that you saw it. The recall influences your decision of whom to call.

Buying a refrigerator is in the middle of the limited decision-making spectrum. If you're lucky, you'll have plenty of time to make a buying decision and it will closely parallel the furniture purchase. If not, it's a disaster requiring an immediate decision, though substantially different than calling a plumber. The plumber is an isolated service and event, whereas you probably have an idea of where you'll go to buy the refrigerator, likely at a retail outlet with which you've had past experience. Once on the showroom floor you will probably encounter brands you recognize and have bought before. In the recent past, when you saw those brands advertised on TV, your mind tallied the fact that the brand in the commercial was the same as the brand in your home. Even if the refrigerator decision must be made quickly, the combination of experience and accumulated external information presents an immediate and viable decision path.

Let's consider what may happen to the routine response behavior of buying a couple of cheeseburgers and fries at Hamburger City. Bubba's been doing that five days a week for years but over time has recognized the need to take better care of himself. His doctor has convinced him to stop smoking, he takes a brisk walk every day, and he's begun to think about his diet. Bubba is unaware of the fact that he's noticed that Hamburger City now sells chicken sandwiches and has unconsciously considered trying one. One lunch hour, all of a sudden, he decides to try a chicken sandwich today. The stimulus for his action, however, is not the menu board at Hamburger City but the signage as he drives by Chicken Heaven, the outlet with the strongest chicken sandwich position in his mind. This action represents a market shift to chicken sandwiches, with Chicken Heaven the beneficiary.

Bob is one of those people who went years with no interest in being popular or interacting with others until he hit a late mid-life crisis and a need recognition began to evolve. In his preliminary, unconscious, information search he immediately ruled out the Gulf Breeze Gentleman's Club, perceiving that relationships developed there would be superficial. Then, as the information search developed into conscious awareness, he realized that true love and meaningful long-term relationships could be attained only through an ostentatious display of material possessions. At that point, he began noticing ads and displays for jewelry, fashion clothing, and exclusive private sports bars. During this phase of susceptibility he was speaking with a colleague, a respected opinion leader on the cutting edge of the local singles scene, who told him, "Bob, no self-respecting person will be seen with you as long as you're driving that '79 Cutlass." This event was the moment at which he began an open conscious information search including marketing-controlled information sources such as manufacturers' websites and non-marketing controlled sources such as car magazines and the Shade Tree Mechanic Show on local access cable.

Evaluation of Alternatives

The evaluation of alternatives begins when information search ends, at least for the time being, and some potential courses of action have been identified. Bob's evoked set, those vehicles under consideration for purchase, had been narrowed down to the Lamborghini Diablo, the Cadillac Cien, and the Roll-Royce Silver Shadow. However, since he is now openly predisposed to making an affirmative buying decision, he is also highly receptive to other alternatives. He might take note of a sharp little Mercedes 2-seater at the local mall or pay special attention to a colleague discussing social events at the Yacht Club. The evoked set expands to include different cars and possible boats. Bob is ready to buy, a dream come true for a salesperson who knows how to engage the prospect and close the sale.

Purchase

Eventually, the prospect either makes a purchase or the process is postponed or discontinued. Bubba, in a break of long-term habit, gets a chicken sandwich at Chicken Heaven. Bob, after an extensive search, test drives the Corvette but, after a quick credit check, the salesperson closes him on a Cavalier. The transaction is over but the customer's experience, which will determine long-term brand loyalty and repeat purchases, has just begun.

Post-purchase Evaluation

Bubba's spur-of-the-moment decision to go to Chicken Heaven was low-risk and of very limited consequence. If he enjoys his lunch and finds the personnel pleasant, he'll return, possibly with increased frequency over time. If his experience is negative, he simply won't go back. Either way, however, there has been a break in his long-term behavior pattern and it will never be the same between him and Hamburger City. Whatever his experience at Chicken Heaven, Bubba is now more amenable to other alternatives. He is more likely to notice the promos for low-fat tacos and chef's salad at Taco Express or the soup and salad bar at Veggie Gardens. His healthy diet need recognition, affirmed in conscious awareness with a purchase decision, has made him a prospect for a wide variety of related alternatives at restaurants and on grocery store shelves. This new behavioral direction many now find him noticing ads for exercise videos and Spike's Gym, commercials which he hadn't even noticed a few months previously.

Bob's purchase was of greater consequence, so he may experience post-purchase tension and anxiety, known in the sales trade as buyer's remorse and among psychologists as cognitive dissonance. Upon initialing the paperwork, he can't help but think "Son of a gun. I can't believe I just dropped twelve grand on a car. I could have bought 24,000 boxes of Pasta Roni for that kind of money." The salesperson, therefore, reassures him about the wisdom of his decision and calls him the next week to thank him again and say how much the dealership is looking forward to its long-term relationship with him. Although Bob's purchase is far more significant than Bubba's, his post-purchase pattern is similar. His unmet needs have been consciously acknowledged and he will begin to notice more of the messages that address those needs. Consistent with his newly-emerging behavior patterns, he may give greater consideration to alternative products with similar extrinsic benefits. He may splurge for a new Timex watch with a stopwatch feature. Then, when networking at Business After Hours, a colleague's compliment about the watch smoothly segues Bob into a comment like, "Yes, the stopwatch feature is very useful for timing my new Cavalier in the quarter mile." This enables him to open a line of conversation about his new car without appearing to be bragging.

Bubba recently bought a new, top-of-the-line TV set, which set him back almost as much as the Cavalier cost Bob. His wife LaVergne, who to this day believes the TV cost less than half what he actually paid for it, nearly had a conniption fit when she saw it. For about a week even Bubba was suffering an occasional twinge of cognitive dissonance. But then he began noticing ads for the set and its manufacturer, dramatized in high definition on his 72-inch screen, and was reassured that he owned a product of the highest quality, an excellent value from the leader in the product category. Bubba's cognitive dissonance began to dissipate and was soon a thing of the past.

Generally, we think of the primary role of advertising as influencing behavior during the information search and evaluation of alternatives. Advertising definitely is important at those stages, but not sufficient to ensure the purchase decision. It is unlikely that Bubba walked into the electronics store knowing the precise brand and model he was going to buy. In fact, it is very possible he had not finalized the decision to buy anything *at all*, though he was certainly predisposed to doing so. When Bubba walked in the door, though he was probably not consciously aware of it, his mind was imprinted with a list of brands that advertised. He probably couldn't have told you much about the differences in advertising among brands he'd seen, and, if asked, likely confused the identity of specific messages among advertised brands. If he had a specific brand and product in mind that inclination was probably influenced by a friend Bubba considered an opinion leader for the electronics category. That friend may have owned the model Bubba came to look at, or Bubba may have been inclined to buy the same brand as his friend but the model next up in the line, wanting to one-up him.

Over the past several years Bubba was more likely to have noticed advertising for his current brand of TV. People have higher advertising awareness for products and brands they own and use than for those they don't. Think about that. The last time you bought a car or major appliance, didn't you suddenly notice how many more of them were owned by others and didn't you suddenly notice or pay more attention to their commercial messages, which seemed to be appearing with greater frequency. Actually, there was nothing sudden about it. You were merely perceiving environmental cues and commercial messages you had not noticed or which had not registered on your conscious mind.

In any case, when Bubba goes into the electronics store, he has a fundamental recognition of brands that advertise and perhaps some inclinations affected by experience, brand loyalty, and opinion leaders. However, his ultimate decision—what he buys, if he buys at all—will be significantly influenced by product presentation at the point of encounter and the professionalism and expertise of the retail salesperson.

Although advertising has an effect on Bubba's purchasing decision, it plays an equally important role during the post-purchase evaluation, alleviating his cognitive dissonance. At this time, when his attention to the manufacturer's commercial messages has been heightened, this provides him the opportunity to glean facts to provide rational justification of what actually was, to a large extent, an emotional decision. Thus, when one of his buddies asks why he bought such-and-such brand and model, he can talk about its innovative technology, quality assurance, and professional endorsements rather than confess the truth: "I don't know what happened. I just took one look at it and had to have it."

For consumer non-durables, low-risk buying decisions among familiar brands, the *primary* effect of advertising is *after* the purchase. As a rule, the objective measurement of advertising effectiveness is ad awareness within the target market. Marketers then strive to achieve a higher-than-standard awareness for a particular budget allocation or to achieve the standard level of awareness at a lesser expense.

I worked with a beverage manufacturer that understood how to maximize the effectiveness of its advertising dollars. In this category an in-store promotion at an attractive price was guaranteed to draw traffic. With a best food day ad feature in the local paper, and a special display—with pricing and point-of-sale—at the point of encounter, a store could expect to sell an additional 1200 cases during a promo week. We found that running advertising for the week preceding such a promotion had no impact on sales during the promo period. When people saw the promo and hot price they bought, advertising notwithstanding. However, when we ran advertising the week *after* the promotion we achieved an inordinately high level of awareness. Just as Bubba had a higher ad awareness of his TV set brand after the purchase, the beverage customers had a higher awareness of the product they had stocked up on during the previous week's promotion. If you market a frequently purchased, low-risk product, you might also discover that your objective of advertising awareness can be more effectively achieved by concentrating your media schedule on the period following heavy promotion rather than preceding it.

Issues of Perception

Selective Exposure

Prospects make decisions affecting which stimuli they will see and not see. For instance, I do not watch network sitcoms nor do I listen to Golden Oldies radio stations. If you advertise through those media you will not reach me, even if I'm in your target market. You may have invested in a prominent billboard on our local interstate spur but it will not be seen by citizens who elect not to use the road while it's under construction. The readership of a special interest magazine may be a perfect reflection of your target market but your full-page color an will not be seen by all those persons who elect not to look at the magazine and are thus not exposed to your message.

Selective Perception

People see what they want to see and expect to see, a function of their interests, value systems, and experiences. Show a commercial featuring a bevy of good-looking people and the heterosexual males in the audience will notice the beautiful women whereas the heterosexual females will notice the hot guys. While walking down a city street an innocent person from the country perceives friends enjoying a conversation, whereas her streetwise counterpart perceives potential predators and changes direction.

Selective perception is the basis of stereotyping and racism. Persons attributing particular characteristics to certain classes of persons will consistently perceive those assigned characteristics in the attendant classes. If someone has stereotyped a class of persons as stupid or lazy he or she will consistently see stupidity or laziness in their members. If you expect to see garbage, you will see garbage.

An offshoot of selective perception is the selective distortion of information that conflicts with one's attitudes or beliefs. Distorting reality helps consumers feed denial of negative information relating to their present lifestyle choices or prior purchase decisions. It permits politicians to believe that disastrous policy decisions are on track, and enables marketing managers to rationalize that a product failure is about to catch on.

People selectively retain information the same way they selectively perceive and distort it. They will tend to remember information and experiences that confirm predisposed attitudes and beliefs, but will conveniently forget anything in conflict. If you believe someone is a crook, you will remember all the facts supporting your position but forget those facts in opposition. Should a person point out a fact demonstrating that individual's integrity, you would distort the fact to perceive manipulation that had only created a false impression of integrity.

All these issues of perception are in play throughout the decision-making process. Marketing managers must not assume that what they see is what customers and prospects see. The marketing landscape is littered with disasters that occurred when promotions or commercial messages were perceived and interpreted in a manner very different than intended. You may be highly confident that the audience will receive the message you send but you'd better check that out thoroughly just to be sure. If you mean to say, "This product is for active mature people," you don't want them to hear, "If you use this stuff, you're old."

"Economic Man" and Extensive Decision-Making

The theoretical concept of "Economic Man" has been around for centuries. In a nutshell, it assumes that man is a rational creature who makes logical choices weighing benefits and value against cost for purchase alternatives. It was a reasonable explanation of behavior in an old economy dominated by tangible products. How much more would you pay for a 16-foot boat made of oak compared to the 12-footer made of pine? Would you rather have a pint of stout ale for two shillings or a pint of watered-down brew for one shilling? What's the price point at which you'll buy your neighbor's cow or sell your cow to him?

There's nothing fundamentally wrong with the essential perspective of the "Economic Man," but modern marketing has gone far beyond decisions evaluating nothing more than specific features and ingredients. Many decisions reflect emotional reactions to intangible cues. The prospect is making a conscious assessment of content-based alternatives and also a qualitative yes-no reaction to a feeling about which he or she may not even be aware.

Let's consider some traditional examples of extensive decision-making: buying a home, or choosing a mate. Both these examples have significant consequences and involve high levels of risk so we would expect them to reflect a complex evaluation of alternatives.

I've bought two houses in the past thirty years and both times knew I was going to buy the place the instant I saw it, before even going inside. In Atlanta it was the one and only house I looked at. In Florida it was the last place I was going to look at after spending an entire week house hunting. Both homes, however, shared similarities in the buying experience. I had limited consideration to traditional middle-class neighborhoods, excluding new developments or subdivisions. On my initial drive down the street I made a quick yes-or-no decision about whether or not I wanted to live on it. Approaching the driveway, I wanted to be certain the house was nestled in a wooded lot and not visible from the street. Thus, I did have specific criteria for assembling my evoked set. However, I never generated a number of alternatives from which to make a rational choice. Suddenly, it was, "Wow! This is it!" Fortunately, I knew enough about negotiation not to let the current owners know my feelings and the fact that I was not going to walk away from the table even if I had to pay the asking price, which I didn't.

On the day he bought the TV set, it's entirely possible that Bubba was not even considering such a purchase as he sipped his morning coffee. His first thought of action may have occurred as he approached the electronics store on the way home from work and even then he may just have been intending to look around. What happened to trigger the buying response? When he first looked at it, was the set showing a NASCAR race that made him feel he was right there in the pits? Was it a comment by the salesperson, painting a picture of Bubba and his buddies watching the big game on Saturday? Who knows? Marketing managers understand that advertising will establish legitimacy and convey some information about a product which, among other cues, may lead prospects to the point of encounter. Then, whether it's a TV set for Bubba or a house for me, they also understand that something in the product presentation must make the prospect think, "Yes."

The decision-making process is remarkably similar for the other major decision: selecting a mate. Few people go through the literal theoretical decision-making model, identifying a number of qualified prospects from which to assemble an evoked set and then selecting the winning candidate. In all my life I have encountered only one person who approached courtship according to the precise extensive decision-making model. He was an economist, who selected a candidate pool of eight women he decided to date, out of which he was determined to ask one to marry him. He never saw his project to fruition, as none of the eight would go out with him, so he bought a cat instead.

Just as in the other examples of extensive decision-making most people have an inclination to meet someone but may not be actively looking. Then, often out of the blue, they meet someone and "it happens." There may have been some essential qualifying characteristics, such as gender and an age over 18 and under 80, but the buying decision was significantly impacted by emotions and product presentation at the point of encounter. Just as advertising helps people justify the wisdom of a decision in post-purchase evaluation, emerging facts about the mate-designate—family background, education, income, and all the rest—help build the illusion that the sudden emotion-laden decision was really the product of logic and deliberation.

If emotions and product presentation at the point of encounter have such a major impact in extensive decision-making, you can readily imagine how much more important they are in routine response behavior and limited decision-making. A convenience store may sell an additional 400 bottles of pop a day merely by placing an on-ice display near the register. Retailers know that product sales off the shelf are in nearly direct proportion to visibility. Reduce the facings from four to two, and sales will be cut nearly in half. Why do you see pricing and point of sale on displays, even at regular price? Because such signage doubles product sales. Marketing managers don't know exactly what goes on in the minds of individual customers at outlet level. They *do* know that visibility and quality of the presentation at the point of purchase will substantially affect sales and that the failure to execute will detract from sales.

I worked for some time with a consumer products company that believed advertising was virtually the sole driver of sales and that customers would search the stores to find their brands, even on the bottom shelf in some obscure location. The competition, on the other hand, appreciated the fact that outlet-level execution was a prime determinant of sales. Over the years the competition fought for space, one facing at a time, concentrating on placing themselves in the most visible locations early in the traffic flow. In time this strategy succeeded in creating a powerful in-outlet presence and sales parity with their previously dominant counterpart. On a regular basis their loyal customers, not specifically intending to purchase that product class that day, just grabbed one of their products and placed it in the buggy, never thinking twice. Occasionally, a customer previously loyal to the competition saw their display, pricing, and point-of-sale and, never thinking about the fact they were making a brand-switching decision, made a shift in their long-term buying behavior.

Some time ago, theoreticians with expertise in decision-making proposed the concept of a "black box" to describe the unexplainable processes taking place in the minds of customers as they made buying decisions. That perspective has fallen out of vogue in recent years, criticized as an admission of ignorance of the buying process. Recently experts armed with sophisticated models and powerful computers have attempted to identify every variable within the black box, trying to quantify each and every influence leading to a predictable outcome. However, marketing professionals care about aggregate behavior and for them the black box is a viable model. What marketing managers care about is, for example, that there are five million people in their target market. Of these five million, three million are exposed to their commercial message and two million are not. Of the three million exposed to their message, 100,000 have top-of-mind awareness, 300,000 have aided awareness, and the rest have no recall. Then, the marketing managers would want to know the respective proportions who would be exposed to their offering at a point of encounter. What *really* counts is how many then think, "Yes" and buy at that point. The adept marketing managers identifies all the conditions which affect the decision at the point of purchase and executes them to perfection. Execution and implement at the point of encounter is *the most important element* of your marketing plan.

Business Decision-Making

The decision-making process for B2B markets is similar to the process for individual consumer markets, though many of its characteristics differ. Business products are defined as those intended to become part of a manufactured product or which are consumed internally by a business in its operations. Before going further, let's address some important points concerning the nature of business products.

Business Products
Some business products would be of little or no use to ultimate consumers until they are utilized in a manufacturing process and converted in form. Examples would include raw materials (crude oil transported to a refinery), processed materials (sheet steel purchased by an automobile manufacturer), and component parts (chips to be used in making personal computers). Many component parts, however, are marketed through both consumer and business channels including such obvious examples as tires and batteries.

Many business products are consumed by the business customer, who is the final user. This would include everything from ball point pens to outsourced professional accounting services, both of which might also be marketed to individual consumers. Thus, it is possible that product and service providers might establish multiple channel systems to serve the different markets. The outsourcer of accounting services might rely on television, direct mail, and Yellow Pages advertising to reach individual customers but would employ a commissioned sales force and professional networking to contact business customers. Furthermore, it is likely there would be a considerable difference in the profile of service needs among individual and business customers. Thus, the outsourcer would have a different business model for the respective segments.

Similarly, the manufacturer of ball point pens might market directly to large business customers but rely on traditional retail outlets and point-of-purchase merchandising for individual consumers. For this product, however, there is a hybrid account, the large chain office supply store frequented by individuals *and* businesses. Businesses that purchase in these accounts might be too small to justify a personal sales call but the products they buy are business products whereas the exact same products purchased by the individual behind them in line are consumer products. That issue, however, is trivial as long as you remember to serve your customer. Selling through the intermediary, your customer is the retailer. Help retailers sell to both *their* individual customers and *their* business customers. Focus on managing channels rather than limiting your focus to an individual/business end-user perspective. If you market through channel intermediaries, that represents B2B marketing to those channel members.

Characteristics of Business Markets

One of the most notable characteristics of business customers, compared to individual customers, is that they are far fewer in number but feature sales that are much higher. Particularly in industries such as semiconductors and agriculture significant numbers of prospects may be found in areas of geographic concentration. Opportunities for services outsourcers tend to be concentrated in metropolitan areas.

In small businesses, there is usually one person—often the owner—who makes the buying decisions. By contrast, in large corporations, there may be no individual empowered to make a decision without running the proposal through a board or committee. Compound that with the fact that in many markets, every vendor in town is trying to get a piece of the big guys. Thus, many marketers of business products and services find their time better spent with up-and-coming small businesses.

B2B marketing is very often conducted through personal selling. Most buyers in business markets, especially those representing retailers, are trained negotiators with all the facts. Do not even think of calling on one of these people, or let anyone represent you, who enters the buying situation with a lesser command of information and expertise in negotiation tactics and processes. If you do, it is guaranteed you will leave profit on the doorstep. That's the buyer's job, after all. It's even worse with small business owners because it's *their* money you're talking about.

Even more than in consumer markets, there are no borders in B2B marketing. It's a global marketplace in which you cannot compete on price against on-line competitors. Instead, your representatives must demonstrate professional competence that helps their customers build their business by enhancing revenue and reducing cost. Build your business model around the principle of identifying channels of opportunity, then developing strategic alliances and partnerships.

The Business Decision-Making Process

With all the difference there are between consumer and business marketing, the steps of the process are the same. It starts with problem recognition, a step much more easily initiated in B2B marketing since it involves personal selling rather than a reliance on advertising to prod the prospect. It may take Bubba a long time to begin thinking about a healthy diet. On the other hand, a skilled salesperson persuades a business prospect to grant an appointment in which he or she can initiate a conversation designed to uncover and confirm unmet needs and dissatisfactions. This direct approach guides the business prospect to overtly gather information, evaluate alternatives, and make a buying decision, logically, rationally, and consciously. With the entire process in the open and face-to-face it might seem there would be no mysterious "black box" at work. But intangibles are in play in all human interactions, even those which on the surface appear to be objective and rational.

In B2B marketing, there's still the same "Wow" factor that made Bubba say "Yes" to the TV and me say "Yes" to the house, only it's often in the intangible form of the representative instead of the tangible form of a product. Just as individuals may vote yes or no to a prospective mate at first sight, a buyer may vote thumbs up or thumbs down to a representative after only a few words, if any, have been exchanged. Their initial impression will lead to selective perception and selective distortion, biasing their interpretation of seemingly objective facts. Post-purchase evaluation of the product or service may be significantly affected by the relationship, which affects the meaning and interpretation of content. The statement, "I couldn't help it. It's not my fault. You can't blame me." may be accepted as a reasonable and satisfactory explanation or viewed as an incompetent person failing to accept responsibility and accountability. There is still something like a "black box" in play but since it is within the context of interpersonal communication it is easier to identify the dynamics and direct prospects toward a desired outcome.

Whether you deal in direct consumer marketing, B2B marketing, or a channel arrangement that is a combination of the two, there is only one acceptable outcome of post-purchase evaluation. The customer says, or at least unconsciously thinks, "I got more than I expected." That's the formula for brand loyalty and long-term relationships essential to a profitable business. You want consumers to choose you even if the competition is on sale. When the other guys approach your business customers you want those customers to think about how well you've treated them and to be reluctant to risk going with that lower-priced alternative, even though it sounds awfully good.

CHAPTER 5

Information for Decision-Making

Good information is essential for managing internal operations as well as the development and implementation of marketing plans. Thanks to technology information is easier to procure and easier to manage than ever before.

Internal Decision Support System

All organizations, even very small businesses, must centralize their internal data in a decision support system (DSS). The DSS, protected by passwords and firewalls, should include all customer information, sales, inventory, financial reports, outlet profiles and distribution data. All internal data should be retrievable from the DSS and no information should be isolated within an individual turf if it is needed by others in the organization. Nothing should be stored on 3X5 cards or legal pads.

Information flows from everywhere throughout the organization into the DSS on an ongoing basis. With all this at their fingertips, marketing managers can call up information to identify market trends all the way down to market, chain, or outlet level. For example, let's say your company markets a product expected to enjoy 15% sales growth this year. After three months, however, sales are up only 10%. Utilizing the DSS a marketing manager determines that the shortfall can be attributed primarily to the Western Region. Going deeper into the data, he isolates this shortfall to two specific chains in Seattle, Spokane, and Portland. With this information the marketing manager can define the problem with local market data, addressing competitive promotions or other issues at outlet level.

The DSS provides a quick read of sales and financial results for

59

promotions and test markets. Instead of waiting weeks or more to get a read on performance managers can answer results day by day, permitting them to make better decisions and to fine-tune programs. If an ad campaign is not producing the expected results it can be modified or eliminated. If a promotional program is achieving unexpectedly good sales it can be quickly expanded into other markets.

A potential shortcoming of the DSS is that it only provides a perspective on the past. That may be of value in making forward-looking decisions but is unlikely to identify breakthrough new product ideas. Relying on the DSS may be tantamount to driving down the marketing highway, steering the car by looking at the rear-view mirror.

Scanner-based Research

I remember the days before scanners when vendors were confident about getting an appointment with the trade because they had syndicated market share data, already six to fifteen weeks old, that buyers were interested in seeing. Today, thanks to scanners, the trade generates sales data instantly and they sell it to the research companies. That "preferred buyer" scanner code on your key ring was not invented to help you save money but to enable the chain to sell data with all the household and demographics profiles you provided on the application. It has also created opportunities for one-on-one marketing, an example of which I recently experienced. A few months ago one of the local chains ran a special of six-pack double roll toilet tissue at an unprecedented low price. Realizing that such a price was unlikely to be repeated any time soon and that my in-home inventory was not subject to spoilage I descended upon the store, bought up an entire end cap, and drove home with the back seat and trunk of the Cutlass filled with seventy-seven six-packs, which I calculate should hold me for about five-and-a-half years. Interestingly enough, in the mail just two weeks later I received a cents-off coupon for milk of magnesia.

The DSS and scanner-based research are examples of data collected on a regular basis. Let's contrast that with marketing research, the focus of the remainder of this chapter. Marketing research is the process of planning, collecting, and analyzing data pertaining to a *specific* marketing decision.

Marketing Research

Stage 1: Problem Definition

The first thing that must be done before conducting marketing research, and often the most difficult step, is defining the problem. As in any performance problem this is a quantification of what is happening contrasted with what should be happening. In the prior segment that was defined as product sales up 10% instead of 15%. As another example, a theater in the mall may have experienced a sudden decline in its audience. Similarly, a fast food chain may find its long-term pattern of growth slowed or reversing.

This is not yet the time for conducting formal research but it might be appropriate to do some exploratory research. That could include getting out and looking around, talking to customers, employees, and channel members, and gathering some readily attainable facts, perhaps doing some competitive intelligence. In the example of the prior segment the marketing manager isolated the problem to specific markets and chains. A logical next step might be to contact field sales reps in those markets to further narrow definition of the problem. The theater, noting that no new competitors had opened in the area, might suspect a problem with its feature films or suspect an emergence of entertainment alternatives. A fast-food chain could look for competitive outlets and promotions, changing trends in diet, or problems in management or product presentation at outlet level.

During Stage 1 the manager may develop preliminary hypotheses of cause-and-effect relationships which subsequent research will either support or refute. A cause-and-effect relationship is one in which the manipulation of an independent variable (X) will cause a predictable change in a dependent variable (Y).

It is absolutely essential to differentiate between cause-and-effect and correlation. There is positive correlation when two variables move up or down simultaneously. There is reverse correlation when a move up in one variable is accompanied by a move down in another. The mere fact that there is correlation between two variables does *not* automatically mean there is a cause-and-effect relationship, however, and many marketing managers have made bad decisions because they failed to properly differentiate between the two.

Let's start with a trivial example. The rooster crows and half an hour later the sun comes up. The events are correlated but no one believes the rooster *causes* the sun to come up. Almost as trivial: there is a positive correlation between the sale of ice cream cones and shark attacks at Daytona Beach, but only a minority of our citizens would advocate the outlawing of ice cream cone sales to prevent shark attacks. A third variable, the weather, affects both ice cream cone sales and the propensity of people to go in the water.

The overall influence of a third variable can create the mistaken impression that two other variables have a cause-and-effect relationship when they are only correlated. Recently, a packaged goods manufacturer was lamenting a steady decline in market share relative to their leading competitor. Consumer research confirmed a comparable decline and competitive gain for the category's brand perceived by the target market as having the best advertising and as being of the highest quality. Management reacted immediately and decisively, launching a new ad campaign and quality control program, neither of which had an appreciable impact. Unfortunately, management was guilty of an erroneous correlation. Perceptions of having the best advertising and being of the best quality were not independent variables driving the dependent variables: sales. There was a third variable, a substantial increase of competitive promotional activity, that was affecting sales. In turn, consumer research was impacted because respondents are more likely to cite the brand last purchased when specifying best advertising and highest quality. My next door neighbor's dog, who at least gets out of the ivory tower once in awhile, could have figured out that competitive promotions were driving everything else.

Stage 2: Research Design

Having identified relevant variables and their possible relationships the marketing manager is ready to plan the research design, determining what questions are to be addressed, what data is needed, and how information is to be collected and analyzed. But before going further look into the DSS and results of exploratory research, which may fully clarify the situation. In our first example, sales in the two chains in Seattle, Spokane, and Portland could have been affected by a dispute with buyers representing chain management, causing products to be de-listed. This fact might isolate the cause of the overall sales decline, making further research unnecessary.

As a next step look into secondary data: existing information from a variety of sources such as governmental agencies, trade associations, news organizations, and special interest groups. In the old days, this would require a day at the library. Now almost all of it is available on-line.

Since secondary data was collected by someone else for a purpose other than addressing your specific concern it may not be sufficient to answer all your questions but it's a starting point and may be helpful in determining what data you'll need to collect on your own and where you need to go to get that data. Be wary of secondary data if it emanates from sources of questionable reliability, particularly organizations advocating biased points of view.

Should your DSS, exploratory research, and analysis of secondary data prove inadequate, you're going to have to collect primary data, initiating the collection of data to address your specific issues. Research data include survey research, observation research, and experiments.

Survey Research

In-home Interviews

In-home interviews generate high quality data in a comfortable setting in which a researcher can discuss and demonstrate a product. Unfortunately, costs for such a research design may be prohibitively high.

You might need to use in-home interviews if elements of the product demonstration cannot be conducted in an alternative environment or if you need considerable time to conduct a private detailed interview. Additionally, this research design enables you to select a sample representative of your target market.

Mall Intercept

A popular alternative to an in-home interview is the mall intercept. You've likely run across these a time or two. With the mall intercept you can still show, tell, and demonstrate, but it must be brief. You will not be able to stop passers-by for the sort of detailed and private discussion possible in the home.

A drawback of the mall intercept is its representivity. The folks hanging out at the mall on a Saturday afternoon are not a random sample of the entire community. That might not be a problem if your objective is to compare vacuum cleaner A and vacuum cleaner B. It might pose a big problem if you need to project sample results to a large universe in which you expect great variability among different market segments.

In the example I noted of a theater experiencing a sudden decline in its audience, they would first investigate the possibility that their feature films were not attracting as many viewers as were their competitors' offerings. If that turned out not to be the problem they might conduct a mall intercept at their location and perhaps at alternative locations to get input from their target market. Such a study might quantify the impact of a game room and teen nightclub at another mall, opening the question of investigating the opportunity to a consider similar operation themselves.

Telephone Interviews
Historically telephone interviews have yielded data of good quality at low cost. However, refusal rates are high and rising as people become less tolerant to such intrusions. Unethical telemarketers, selling under the guise of research, have undermined the efforts of legitimate researchers. It is prudent to wonder whether certain people, amiables with time on their hands, are more likely to agree to a telephone interview and whether such persons are representative of the population as a whole. Additionally, an inordinate number have an unlisted cell phone and not a listed land line. This point will be discussed in detail later in the chapter.

One thing you can say for telephone interviews is that they yield quick results and an immediate read on emerging trends. For political campaigns and volatile markets experiencing rapidly changing conditions, telephone interviews can provide actionable information overnight.

Mail Surveys
Mail surveys have the advantage of low cost but, on the other side of the coin, they tend to have low data quality due to the fact that certain segments of the population are more likely to respond. This survey bias, known as nonresponse error, was also noted as an emerging issue in

telephone surveys because of the increasing numbers of persons unwilling to participate in the interview.

Persons willing to complete a mail questionnaire may have very strong feelings on one side or the other of the issue being addressed. This is the same bias found among callers to radio talk shows or respondents to e-surveys conducted on TV programs.

E-mail Interview/Computer Disk by Mail

The survey techniques of e-mail interviews or sending a computer disk by mail are alternatives to telephone interviews and mail surveys respectively. They exhibit the same limitations as their respective counterparts, compounded by samples that may be less representative of the total population. Thus, they are most appropriate for B2B research or specific target markets.

Focus Groups

Focus groups are loosely structured open-ended interviews in which six to ten people sit around and discuss product categories, concepts and closely related marketing applications and issues. These groups are most useful at the preliminary stages of strategic development, designed to identify issues to be explored and addressed by further research and product development. Discussions are led by a moderator who guides the conversations, keeps them on track, and encourages participants to get involved and contribute their opinions and input to points being raised. It is imperative that the moderator be neutral and neither lead nor bias the discussion.

Focus groups are relatively inexpensive and simple to conduct. Thus, organizations of all types and sizes, marketing a wide variety of products and services, employ them extensively. I've had personal experiences with focus groups, both as a participant and as a marketing manager contracting for them, and always felt somewhat uncomfortable about their objectivity. I wondered whether, intentionally or not, the moderator was influencing the direction and outcome. Problems encountered in a study conducted by a major research university have intensified my reservations.

The university in question was conducting a study attempting to communicate with autistic children previously unable to express thoughts verbally or in written form. They utilized facilitators who attempted to established contact with the children by gently holding them by the wrist and letting subjects communicate by touching letters prominently displayed on a large panel similar to a typewriter board. The objective of this study was to determine whether these children, previously uncommunicative, could convey messages by tapping out words with those panel letters.

At first, results seemed encouraging. Several of the children, who had never before uttered or written a word, tapped them out on the keyboard. One mother, in tears of joy, proclaimed that her child, in his first words ever expressed, had said he loved her. But soon doubts about the study's breakthroughs began to arise, particularly as some of the children were noted to communicate with perfect spelling and grammar. When one child was purportedly writing poetry, organizers of the study began fearing that something was amiss. To confirm the study's tentative findings researchers employed a double-blind procedure, something that should have been done at the very beginning of the project. Here's how that techniques works. In a single-blind procedure both the child and the facilitator would be shown a picture of a cat. The child would be asked "What's that?" and would proceed to tap out C—A—T on the keyboard. In the double-blind only the child and not the facilitator is shown the picture. Guess what happened. Nothing! Embarrassed researchers discovered that the children were not communicating at all. Everything was coming from the supposedly unbiased facilitators!

This university and all persons organizing this study were of total integrity. There was no question about the objectivity of the facilitators, who were shocked to learn they had been leading the respondents. The results of the double-blind, however, left no doubt that the research design was flawed and its tentative conclusions invalid.

If facilitator bias can invalidate a major research study, consider what it may do to focus groups. Intentionally or not moderator bias may determine the conclusions of your focus group.

Observation Research

If the objectives of your research are to note actions that are observable, and you do not require input from respondents, you might be able to employ observation research, either watching people or tabulating finite events. People may be watched by other persons or video cameras and finite events can be tabulated by persons or machines.

Watching People

There are two common forms of observation research watching people. The first form involves watching subjects' behavior without their knowledge, perhaps using a one-way mirror, an example of which is research conducted by toy companies. They will place young children in a room full of toys and watch their behavior to see what they're interested in playing with and exactly how, and for how long, they play with particular toys. Similarly, at an adult level, researchers will watch shoppers' behaviors in a retail store, observing shopping patterns in a product section, noting such things as the number of alternative brands they pick up to look at and how much time they spend reading labels.

The second form of observation research watching people is mystery shoppers. By employing them an organization hopes to gain an appreciation of the customer's experience at the point of encounter. Car dealerships might utilize them to gauge the attentiveness and professionalism of their sales force. A hotel might want to see how employees handle a demanding and overbearing guest.

In the example of the fast food chain experiencing a reversal of sales growth, they might first conduct a preliminary investigation of trends in eating habits, making a comparative assessment of their menus compared to those of the competition. As a next step consumer research might investigate the target market's assessment of their food and their restaurants. If such research suggests that the target market thinks the food is all right but doesn't like their outlets it might be time to send in the mystery shoppers. This is exactly what happened recently with a major fast food chain. Fighting for profits in a highly competitive industry the chain had cut staff to the point where the properties had become litter-strewn, inside and outside, and were falling below standard for cleanliness in the seating areas and restrooms. The problem was addressed immediately and aggressively, resulting in sales patterns returning to trend.

Tabulating Finite Events

Tabulating events is the less sophisticated type of observation research. Rather than study subjects and their behavior it merely counts events. A human observer might tabulate traffic flow in a retail outlet to determine prime locations or a machine, in the form of a wire across a road, could count the number of vehicles that are exposed to a billboard at a particular location.

Experiments

As the name implies, experiments employ the scientific method in an attempt to discover cause-and-effect relationships. This is achieved by holding all variables constant except the ones being manipulated—the independent variables—and assessing the impact of the manipulation on a dependent variable, often sales. Generally an experiment will manipulate only one independent variable so as to attain an unambiguous read of its impact. It is feasible to manipulate multiple independent variables and evaluate their impacts through analysis of variance calculations but doing so introduces the phenomenon of interactions among variables. The examples I cited earlier about the impact of changing facings, or adding pricing and point-of-sale to a display, were generated through experiments conducted by retail trade groups manipulating one variable at a time in experiments at outlet level.

A common form of experiment is the "mock store," often featuring a very limited selection of product items, perhaps those of only one product category. Subjects are given a line of credit and allowed to choose whatever they want for their allocation. By manipulating prices and product selection in successive waves of the study, researchers get a preliminary feel of the impact of the variables being manipulated. However, data from a mock store are not projectable to the total real-world marketplace and this procedure is not a viable substitute for test marketing.

Stage 3: Sample Selection

Having determined the research procedure appropriate to your needs, the next step is to select the sample to be studied. The first question to be answered at this stage is: what is the universe, the total population of interest from which the sample is to be drawn? As a rule, the universe will be a reflection of the target market to be addressed. It may be very narrow: men 24–39 with incomes over $100,000, having intermediate to advanced skiing skills, living in a six-county metropolitan area. By contrast, the universe may be very broad: a national poll of likely voters in a presidential election.

It is imperative that the sample, the subset of the target population drawn for study, be representative of the universe although far fewer in number. For example, for a poll of registered voters we might use a sample of 2000 households attained through a random dialing of listed telephone numbers. Such a sample is not an *exact* reflection of the universe. Not all voters have a phone or a listed phone. However, for a national political poll, a telephone survey is probably the only practical survey method. Researchers would have to accept error resulting from differences among voters not having phones or refusing to participate in the survey. However, they could address differences among households with unlisted numbers by specifying the population to be surveyed "working telephone numbers" instead of "listed residential telephone numbers." Such a decision would increase survey costs since some of the numbers contacted would be businesses. Thus, more attempts would be needed to attain the desired sample size.

An emerging concern for telephone surveys is the increasing number of individuals who have only a cell phone and not a land line, particularly among younger single people. Researchers must consider whether "working telephone numbers" includes *all* numbers or just land lines. Further complicating the issue is the likelihood that an inordinate number of cell phones would be for businesses, increasing survey costs because an even higher proportion of contacts would be unusable. Add to that the complication arising from the fact that some persons have both a land line and a cell phone. Therefore, if you chose a population to be surveyed as *all* numbers, those persons with both types of phones would have a higher likelihood of being contacted. To the extent that those persons differ from the universe as a whole, error would be introduced to your sample results.

The sample will be more representative if it is a probability sample, one in which every element in the universe has a known non-zero likelihood of being selected. For example, let's say you wish to survey a universe of 102,000 registered voters in Escambia County, 50,000 of which are men and 52,000 women. You randomly select 250 men out of the universe of 50,000 males and 250 women out of the universe of 52,000 females. Thus, every male registered voter in Escambia County has a probability of 250 divided by 50,000 of being selected and every female has a probability of 250 divided by 52,000.

In a random sample, which is a form of probability sample, every element in the universe has an *equal* likelihood of being selected. In the example above there was a random sample among men and a random sample among women. However, since their total population was slightly smaller, each individual man had a slightly higher probability of being selected than each individual woman. For that survey to be a random sample every element of the population would have a probability of 500 divided by 102,000 of being selected. Because of the different numbers of men and women in the universe such a procedure would expect to draw 255 women and 245 men.

If you really want to split hairs and get technical about it there may be no chance of attaining a 100% pure random sample because it may be virtually impossible to assure that every element of the universe has the exact same likelihood of being selected and then contacted. However, you may have good reason to believe that a random sample of all working telephone numbers covers a very large proportion of the total universe. Furthermore, to account for persons who are not at home during the day you might make repeated attempts at different times of the day and week to contact a subject at a selected number and have a specific procedure determining to whom you talk in each household contact. The result will be the minimization of sample error, even though it is not possible to *eliminate* sample error.

The contrast to a probability sample is, aptly enough, a non-probability sample, in which no attempt is made to reach every element of the universe. Such a convenience sample might be selected because it is readily available and researchers are confident it will be sufficiently representative to provide satisfactory data. For example, you might wish to do a survey of small businesses with the population to be surveyed chosen from a list of members of the Chamber of Commerce. You know that not every small business belongs to the Chamber but you're confident that its membership list will provide actionable information of satisfactory validity.

Along these lines, there might be a burning issue on campus and I could survey students in my classes to gauge their opinions. Such a procedure would not be as representative as an e-mail survey of every student on campus but it might tell me what I need to know. Such a sample would be biased to the extent that juniors and seniors majoring in Business may not reflect the campus at-large but if I discovered that none of my 180 students were aware of a legislative initiative in the State House of Representatives I would be confident that the total student body probably didn't know much about it, either. By contrast, it would not be reasonable to believe I could get a valid read of campus opinions on abortion by only sampling very liberal or very conservative political action groups.

Stage 4: Collect and Analyze Data
Finally, having determined the population of interest and research method, you go to the field, collect data, and conduct the analysis. At this stage it is essential to understand various types of errors will affect the validity of the findings, despite the best efforts in sample selection and research design. I've touched on some of these concerns throughout this chapter. Let's now address them in detail.

Marketing Research Errors

Erroneous Causal Links
It is essential to differentiate between correlation and cause-and-effect. As illustrated in earlier examples do not assume a cause-and-effect relationship before conducting an experiment in which the purported independent variable is isolated and manipulated.

Random Error
You will always encounter random error when sampling a target population as your sample cannot and will not be a perfect representation of the universe. Random error is what you see in political polls, where data are quoted with a "margin of error of such-and-such percent." For example, you will see a president's popularity as 60%, plus or minus 3%. What that means is that the survey has determined that the "best estimate" of popularity is 60%. There's a 50-50 chance that

it's either under 60% or over 60%. The margin of error of plus or minus 3% means that there's a 95% probability that the true measure is somewhere in the range of 57% to 63%. That is to say, there's a 5% probability that the true measure is either less than 57% or over 63%. Due to pure random chance, occasionally your survey is off the mark.

Margins of error are primarily a function of sample sizes and only secondarily are affected by the size of the universe. It requires almost as large a sample to attain a certain margin of error for the State of Florida as it does for the entire nation. Therefore, it is not possible to break out small subsets of samples without incurring unacceptably large margins of error. To generate valid state-by-state data you must take a sample large enough for the desired margin of error in each state, remembering that the sample size for Wyoming will need to be nearly as large as that for California. Then you can build *up* to a national sample by weighting each state in proportion to its total population. I recall one company that was conducting consumer surveys in metropolitan areas, with a sample size adequate for a reasonable margin of error in their total sample. However, they then proceeded to break down the sample by sex and by age ranges as narrow as five years. Sample sizes for, say, girls between eight and twelve were so small as to be totally meaningless, but they still made marketing decisions using those data.

Sampling Error

There is a sampling error when a sample differs from the population of interest. This was the problem cited in the choice of listed telephone numbers to sample the universe of registered voters or relying on call-ins to talk shows to be representative of the population as a whole, effects similar to those of nonresponse error. In all surveys researchers should carefully consider the extent to which sampling error will affect the validity of the findings. A telephone survey may tell you what you need to know about voters' attitudes. Don't expect that procedure to tell you much about attitudes of the homeless.

Measurement Error

In certain circumstances, you will have measurement error because information provided by respondents is unreliable. Either they cannot be depended on to do what they say they're going to do or they purposely lie to you. A classic example of the former are "intention to buy" questions you might ask at the end of a demonstration conducted at home or in a mall intercept. Don't make sales forecasts or plan production runs based on the results, which are always inordinately high. Maybe people really mean it when they say they intend to buy your product or maybe they're just telling you what you want to hear.

The latter situation, in which respondents purposely lie to you, will be encountered when you begin infringing on private or personal actions and beliefs. In the last week, I've heard separate reports claiming that alcohol use among high school kids is up and that it is down. Which one is right? Who knows, since the data were obtained by interviewing the kids themselves. I remember the day when kids who drank would deny it if asked by a researcher. Today, it's entirely possible that kids might claim they do drink even if they don't. Social changes and measurement error make these data of dubious reliability.

Non-Projectability of Data

I've saved this one for last because it's the worst. Non-projectability of data, also known as a lack of external validity, occurs when the results of a study do not reflect what happens in the real world. You can do everything right in survey procedure, sample selection, and collect data in an entirely proper and unbiased manner, but the results will be misleading. An example of this, a classic marketing disaster, occurred when a major brewer considered a new manufacturing process that would reduce production time and costs considerably. They conducted extensive taste tests on old formula versus new formula, comparing their alternative products vis-à-vis the competition, and found the products indistinguishable. All internal research procedures were valid. They rotated the order of products being sampled. *No one* could tell the difference. Until, that is, they changed the process and placed the new product on the shelf, at which time its users cried out in a collective "Yuk!" What happened under controlled conditions in their study was not predictive of what happened when their loyal users drank a six-pack of the stuff on Saturday night. The brand never recovered.

There's no substitute for having the facts, with actionable information at your fingertips. With this information you're ready to decide who to target and plan for marketing to them.

CHAPTER 6

Segmenting and Targeting Markets

So far, I've described marketing and its role in the organization, issues related to the external environment, the basics of buyer behavior, and information for decision making. That's the foundation of everything else I'll discuss from this point forward. Now it's time to consider whom to target, with what product or service, and the process of developing a comprehensive marketing strategy.

Earlier I noted the need to create points of differentiation for any product or service, to make it special in some way, creating value worth paying for compared to a basic commodity. Now, we must ask: Special for whom? Who is it you desire to target and what are the points of differentiation important to that target market?

Market Segmentation

Market segmentation is the process of dividing a large market of dissimilar customers and prospects into a number of smaller markets with similar customers and prospects. Seldom, if ever, is there a large homogeneous market, one of similar customers and prospects to be addressed.

A large homogeneous market tends to be one for a totally undifferentiated commodity, consummate examples of which would be electricity and water. But even those products present an opportunity for segmentation. Everyone needs electricity but some smaller market segments might be targets for alternative forms of power generation or alternative forms of energy to replace a portion of their present dependence on electricity. Similarly, everyone needs water but some market segments would have an interest in water softening and purification. In sum, for any product or service addressing a customer need it is possible to identify and address one or more smaller sub-segments that will respond favorably to particular forms of differentiation. For marketers there's an opportunity to create value to satisfy needs of those smaller segments. The key questions are: On what basis will you break down the total market into smaller segments with similar needs? And: Out of all the unique segments identified, which ones will you address, with what, and how? This is not a one-time process but must be done on a regular basis, probably in developing an annual strategic plan. The world, customers and prospects, and competitive alternatives change at an increasing rate. Today's givens may be next year's outdated assumptions.

Starting Point: Select a Market

The starting point and perhaps most difficult step in market segmentation is the selection of a market for consideration. If you define a market as a particular product class you risk taking a production orientation and approaching that market from the perspective of your present product mix, not customer needs. Remember the earlier example of perceiving a narrow market for books instead of the broader customer-focused market for information. On the other side of the equation, you must consider the capabilities and limitations of your organization. If you have a differential advantage in the production of books—a modern facility on which there is no outstanding debt—you may have a valid rationale in pursuing new opportunities in book publishing, even as your explore emerging opportunities in technology-based information.

Similarly, it may be proper to define your business as furniture rather than the broader definition of home furnishings if related products such as lamps and rugs are outside your sphere of expertise and manufacturing capability. Rather than address those ancillary markets directly it might be more appropriate to develop strategic alliances with manufacturers of related products, working together to secure distribution through retail channels.

It makes sense for large consumer products companies to adopt a narrower product class focus initially. Procter & Gamble has been extremely successful in the toothpaste market. Toothpaste is a product used by almost everyone and they have developed numerous products to address the specific needs of sub-segments of the toothpaste market.

It might be outside P&G's interest or capability to define their market as dental cleaning products and expand into the area of electric or battery-operated tooth cleaners. However, it was within organization parameters to address the tooth-whitening market with White Stripes.

Chances are good that it will be appropriate to define your market more broadly, and in terms of a customer need, if your organization can readily adapt itself to address those emerging needs. In cases of rapidly-changing market conditions it may be essential to radically change market definitions or perish. Yes, you may be able to hold onto the narrow definition of the book market. No, you will not survive if you retain a perspective of the camera film market.

It's been very interesting to watch one of our local entrepreneurs modify the definition of his market in recent years. Twenty years ago Butch Biceps had a roaring business over at Butch's Sports Bar. It was *the* place to go for all the hard-working hard-drinking men and women in the neighborhood: pitchers and longnecks of beer, salty snacks and pickled eggs at the bar. But then society began to change. It was no longer acceptable to drink and drive and folks began to be concerned about the consequences of hooking up with someone they met at a low-class dive. After a couple of years of declining revenues Butch got the message and re-defined his market as the restaurant business. He put in a kitchen and introduced a menu of steaks, catfish, and burgers, cleaned the place up, and added a seating area and big-screen TV. The crowds and total revenue increased even though beer sales were less than half what they used to be. Then a couple of years ago the state banned smoking in restaurants. Instead of moaning about the ban hurting business, Butch recognized the opportunity to re-define his business as family entertainment and dining. The place is now Butch's Family Sports Emporium, featuring a huge kid's room with video games and an alcohol-free family seating section. Any seat in the house has a view of at least five wall-sized TV's showing everything from football to extreme sports. Just down the road he's opened Butch's Back Room, a low-over-head dive for the niche market beer and cigarette crowd. It's nothing like the old days, but it's still a viable market segment. Butch's point of differentiation is a partnership with his brother Tiny, who runs the cab company. For ten bucks Tiny gives you a cab ride to and from Butch's Back Room and that includes your first two pitchers of beer.

Qualifying Standards for Segmentation

There are four standards a segment must meet. It must be viable, identifiable/measurable, accessible, and uniquely responsive.

Viable

To be viable a proposed segment must have sufficient potential to justify targeting it. That means there must be prospects with an interest in the product and the means to purchase it. There would appear to be no point in marketing new cars to 14-year-olds but 8th graders could be viable prospects in four or five years and marketers might wish to create a positive brand image in those future buyers at an early age. In product classes such as alcohol or tobacco the question of viability presents serious ethical concerns. By the time prospective customers become legally viable they will have already established brand preferences even though they may not have yet tried the product. I was very interested to note, as I did my run through the neighborhood the other day, a group of nine-year-olds parroting words of the commercial positioning line from a popular beer's advertising.

On the other end of the scale, 55-year-olds might not be viable prospects for a Medicare supplement but marketers might perceive a need to establish brand awareness some time before those persons enter the prospect pool. Similarly, a hospital specializing in cancer treatment would want to establish its position in a prospect's mind *before* that prospect was diagnosed with cancer.

A segment may be viable with only one prospect in the total market, examples of which include one-of-a-kind products such as mining equipment or highly specialized legal services. Conversely, a segment may not be viable even though numerous persons would be interested in the product if potential sales are too low to be profitable. Fast food companies discovered this to be the case with low-calorie pizza.

Identifiable/Measurable

You will have a difficult time determining whether a segment is viable, let alone market to it, if you cannot find some means of identifying prospects and measuring how many of them there are. For example, a social services agency might be considering offering treatment and counseling to elderly persons who are slipping into patterns of alcohol abuse. They may have anecdotal information that many seniors, with little to do all day, steadily increase alcohol consumption to the point where it becomes a health problem, but the agency has no reliable means of quantifying the size of the market or generating a list of persons who would benefit from their services. Along those same lines, a pharmaceutical company may be considering the introduction of a breakthrough product to treat high cholesterol. However, many persons in the population, very probably including a disproportionally high number of those who could benefit from the drug, never see a doctor to get a cholesterol screening. The pharmaceutical company will have difficulty estimating market potential for their new product, let alone getting through to much of its target market.

Accessible
Closely related to the standard of being identifiable and measurable, a segment must be accessible: that is, you must be able to reach it with your message. The social services agency may be able to get through to its elderly prospects with public service announcements (PSAs) on radio and TV and through print media read by its target market. However, they may encounter considerable difficulty attempting to access another target market: the homeless. The agency may have job training and alcohol/drug treatment programs that would benefit their target market but be unsuccessful attempting to communicate with them.

Responsive
Unless the target market responds to your message you're dead in the water. Remember, though, that a satisfactory response may be nothing more than a vague memory that "this brand advertises," the value of which is realized with product presentation at the point of encounter. Additionally, you do not expect recall, let alone direct action, from every member of the target segment. A campaign could be considered successful if a very small proportion of the elderly slipping toward a drinking problem or of the population not having cholesterol screening were to notice the message and take action. Those persons, with whom marketers gain the first foothold into a segment, are likely to influence other persons in similar circumstances. When Faye Dowdey begins to notice she's

starting in on the wine earlier and earlier in the day, she's not only more likely to pay increasing attention to the agency's message but also likely to bring up the issue with friends in similar circumstances. When Bubba checks his cholesterol and discovers he was "this close" to real trouble you can bet he'll tell his buddies at Butch's Family Sports Emporium.

Each proposed segment must respond differently or there is no justification for treating it as a separate segment. If there is no difference in response between two proposed segments, one for ages 25–29 and the other for ages 30–34, they should be combined into a single segment of ages 25–34.

If you determine that a proposed target market can be broken into segments which meet the qualifying standards, the next step is to determine those bases on which the market will be segmented. I'll first address traditional segmentation bases, then extrinsic bases. Effective marketers employ both traditional and extrinsic bases, each complementing the other.

Traditional Segmentation Bases

Product Features/Benefits

The most fundamental form of segmentation is the offering of products and services with different features, and attendant benefits. Implicit in this strategy is that particular features will be important to specific segments. Let's consider toothpaste: Brand A has a taste kids love and it prevents cavities so it's targeted toward moms to buy for their young children; Brand B gives you fresh breath and whitens your teeth and is aimed at young people in the social scene; Brand C controls tartar for adults interested in good dental health; and Brand D helps prevent gum disease and is targeted at the folks in fear of impending dentures.

Motel chain A has a basic room, period; Motel chain B has a bit nicer room, with a free continental breakfast; Motel chain C has a big room, king-size bed, 25-inch TV, free Internet access, and a full breakfast buffet; Motel chain D has all that with a suite and free cocktail hour. Along the target market continuum the benefits address the needs of those on a budget looking for a low price all the way up to an executive on expense account.

Benefit segmentation is the most basic point of differentiation. It adds something to an undifferentiated commodity and distinguishes a product from the competition. As I noted in the examples of toothpaste and motel chains, different benefits are important to different target markets. Under a marketing orientation, you would start by identifying the most important segments and the benefits most important to each segment.

Geography

This one's a no-brainer: some product categories are better developed in certain regions of the country than in others. Per-capita spending for snowmobiles is higher in Mankato than in Pensacola but we've got them beat for cheese grits. A franchise for solar hot water heaters will be more lucrative in Yuma than in Syracuse. Mom, bless her, returned from a cruise to Alaska to report that the temperature had never risen above 60 in Juneau even though she was there in July. It was a good thing it hadn't been warmer, she said, as the hotel didn't have air conditioning and there wasn't even an air conditioning contractor in town.

If you're considering opening a place to sell cheese steaks you might first think about locating in Philly. But maybe not. A point I'll address in marketing strategy is the idea of addressing markets not dominated by entrenched competition. The best approach could be to locate in an untapped market where you can establish category leadership. Consider selling cheese steaks in Pittsburgh, though you should pass on air conditioning systems in Juneau.

Demographics

Many marketers segment their business by demographics. That's logical because certain products would be of interest *only* to specific demographic segments. Denture cleanser is for older people, bubble gum for kids. Top-end luxury cars are marketed to people in the higher income brackets, diapers to people with young children.

Demographic segmentation may be necessary but it is never sufficient. To segment solely on demographics is to assume that all persons in the category are alike, inconsistent with a marketing orientation. Not all African-Americans, Hispanics, or men 24–39 can be addressed with the same message. Thus, although demographics may be a segmenting variable, it cannot be the *only* segmenting variable.

Usage Rate

There's something to be said for concentrating efforts on those consumers who are the category's heavy users. The 80–20 rule, also known as the Pareto Principle, predicts that 20% of your customers will account for 80% of your sales. However, if you fail to describe those heavy users beyond demographic descriptors the usage rate variable may not be useful. Of course 80% of the sales for denture cleanser are older persons. Of course 80% of beer is consumed by young males. And of course single-person households don't buy a lot of baby food. Without extending the heavy-user profile beyond demographics you will not be able to market to them effectively. However, it may be possible to isolate those heavy users, learn more about them, and identify extrinsic variables we can put to use. Effective marketers segment and target markets with extrinsic variables that reflect and complement the traditional variables.

Extrinsics and Marketing

Extrinsic variables are, by definition, those which are outside the product per se. You didn't see much of them in the early days of marketing, when messages focused primarily on the product, what it did, and why it was superior to the competition. Brand A shampoo leaves your hair fresh and clean, *and* controls dandruff. Brand B cake mix has more chocolate and takes less time to fix. Or Brand C automobile comes with a V-8 and has more power. Today many advertising messages say little or nothing about the product, concentrating primarily on the extrinsics. In the lingo of the professional salesperson, you translate product features into customer benefits and personalize the benefits. The marketing concept is built upon the idea of focusing on benefits most important to the customer. That means extrinsics!

So, use Brand A shampoo and you'll meet someone interesting tonight at the mosh pit. Buy Brand B cake mix because your kids will love you for it. And own a Brand C automobile because it will be a tangible symbol of your success, or because your family will be safer, or because you're proud to be an American—whatever.

Extrinsic Segmentation Bases

Extrinsic segmentation bases take us beyond the traditional bases of demographics and large-scale geography, instead defining markets based upon how people see themselves, which is a good predictor of products and services they will be interested in and what messages they will respond to. Effective marketing managers recognize that segmentation by extrinsic variables will identify persons who are heavy users in a product category and what benefits they are seeking. Furthermore, segmenting by extrinsics helps you to determine the appropriate message and its execution. Product benefits and extrinsic segmentation bases are the dog, and product features and traditional segmentation bases are the tail. Don't lose sight of which should be wagging which.

Lifestyle

Marketers approach extrinsic segmentation through an assessment and categorization of lifestyles predominantly by evaluating attitudes, interests, and opinions (AIOs). Additionally, it is helpful to identify a person's reference groups and opinion leaders, all of whom influence an individual's AIOs and purchasing behavior.

For a marketer information about small informal primary membership groups is not particularly useful. Products and services you buy, benefits sought, and brand loyalty are all heavily influenced by your family, friends, and local groups you belong to but information about them is at too small a scale to be actionable. More useful are larger formal groups such as Greenpeace, the National Organization for Women, the Southern Baptist Convention, or the Republican Party. It is not all that important whether these are membership groups—a person actually belongs to them—or aspirational groups, which the individual relates to and desires to emulate. Also useful are informal groups that relate to a lifestyle. This could include aspirational groups, ones admired by the individual—surfers, pop music stars, or professional golfers—or nonaspirational groups—ones the individual wants nothing whatsoever to do with. Certain informal groups, such as Army commandos or special issues advocates, could be aspirational among persons of one lifestyle and nonaspirational among those of a different lifestyle.

Opinion leaders are individuals, often affiliated with a person's reference groups or informal aspirational groups, who influence others' opinions. They would include national talk show hosts, leaders of political or special interest organizations, and individual sports or media celebrities.

Marketers have discovered that persons with similar reference groups and opinion leaders tend to have similar AIOs and lifestyles, share similar media and buying behavior, and respond favorably to certain messages promoting similar extrinsics. Thus, firms with a marketing orientation focus on those variables as segmentation bases.

Only a couple of decades ago lifestyle was nearly synonymous with a person's demographic profile, particularly age, family status, and income. College-educated professionals, disproportionally white and male, were expected to marry and start a family in their late 20s or early 30s. There were certain neighborhoods they were expected to live in, specific products and brands they were expected to display, wear, and drive. They were expected to have narrowly defined attitudes, interests, and opinions, and affiliate themselves with designated organizations in the community. College-educated women were patronized in staff positions, ostensibly until they found a husband and assumed a primary role of housewife and caretaker. The workplace and neighborhoods were predictable and homogenized. Alternative lifestyles were unthinkable and few persons deviated from the norm. Segmenting markets was easy and basic.

The Emergence of Diversity

Television and the struggle for individual rights have changed our society. Technology has changed the world. Business professionals have learned that survival in today's highly competitive marketplace is possible only by hiring persons who demonstrate the highest levels of objective, measurable performance. No one has the luxury of maintaining a good-old-boy network subsidizing any individual or demographic groups. Diversity has emerged in the organization and in the marketplace, each building on the other. Organizations recognize the need to market to these emerging segments and appreciate the fact that they cannot do so with management comprised solely of white, Anglo-Saxon, heterosexual, male Protestants.

America is no longer the melting pot. It's more like minestrone soup. Just as diversity has emerged in the workplace we see great variability and diversity of life outside the organization. No longer are one's social life, AIOs, and lifestyle defined by the organization. Individual employees may have friendships with persons associated with many different firms, from various social and cultural backgrounds, sharing a common interest in everything from bird watching to rollerblading. Married and unmarried couples living together pursue their own professional careers with neither of them feeling social ties to the other's organization.

The communication revolution has exposed us all to people and perspectives that previous generations didn't even know existed. I know this dates me, but I can remember when the only thing to do on a summer afternoon was to listen to a baseball game on the radio. Today you can see surfing, auto racing, diving, pee-wee hockey, and everything in between—in living high-definition color on your 72-inch screen. People don't want to conform to some narrowly-defined life with traditional boundaries. They want to "be me" and express themselves as individuals even if in doing so they look and act remarkably similar to the million other followers of their rock star opinion leader.

Component Lifestyles

Today, many persons associate themselves with a number of component lifestyles, each of them having important implications for purchasing behavior. John is a business executive, marathon runner, and NASCAR dad. Sarah is a sales professional, community activist, and scuba diver. Every season John buys three or four travel packages with groups visiting various cities to see NFL games. Sarah is a patron of the arts and belongs to a group that travels to New York for long weekends of the theater and symphony. Together, they and the kids go on camping and hiking trips to the mountains or diving trips to the shore. These various component lifestyles add up to a significant proportion of their discretionary income.

Culture and Subcultures

A culture is defined by consistent patterns of values and attitudes, norms and behavior. Implicit in the concept are long-term cultural inclinations to use certain products and services, and consistent responses to media styles and messages. Generally, so-called "American culture and values"—hard work, thrift, patriotism, and individual competitive struggle—are too broad to be applied universally. However, that message plays perfectly to the sub-suburban and rural middle class subculture. Beyond that no marketer ever went wrong affiliating themselves with tradition and the flag, especially at holidays commemorating those who served and sacrificed.

There are examples of subcultures that can be defined demographically. Immediately coming to mind are first-generation immigrants who do not speak English, have not been integrated into the general population, and who live within narrowly-defined geographic boundaries. Additionally, marketers define young children as a target market subculture classified solely by age. Cereal manufacturers targeting a product to kids under six have no need to sub-segment the demographic. Execution consists of featuring the product on the bottom shelf where kids recognize it even if they're too young to read and begin clamoring "Oh, mommy!"

Beyond young children, however, generalizing solely on age is false collectivization. Terms like "Baby Boomers," "Gen X," and "Gen Y" are demographic traps. Persons in those groups are not all alike and must be further segmented by extrinsics.

If you can define a subculture solely by demographics, all well and good. Just don't expect that to happen often. Generally you will be defining a subculture as a segment of persons sharing similar component lifestyles. Such subcultures feature persons with similar AIOs, purchasing patterns, and responsiveness. Furthermore, persons within a subculture tend to congregate in neighborhoods of like-minded others and have closely-related media habits, a marketer's dream.

Geodemographics

Geodemographic segmentation is the process of breaking down a marketing area into neighborhoods of persons with similar lifestyles. These neighborhoods tend to reflect similar demographics among their respective residents but, more importantly, similar benefit and usage bases that can be addressed with similar intangible cues, advertising themes, and extrinsics through similar media outlets. Geodemographics are a more effective segmentation strategy than demographics alone and can help you avoid the demographic trap. Let's look at a couple of examples that illustrate the point.

Twenty years ago, an old neighborhood in a major city had fallen victim to stagnation. Traditional light-manufacturing businesses in the area had closed and a large number of the once stately homes were falling into disrepair. Then, young professionals—singles and couples, gender-mixed—began moving in and restoring the properties. Soon the area was undergoing gentrification. Restaurants, clubs, coffee shops, and boutiques opened and enjoyed a thriving business. The area came alive and property values were on the upswing. Although most of the neighborhood's households consist of single persons or couples without children, about one household in eight is a traditional family of mom, dad, and kids. Looking only at demographics you would aggregate those traditional families with their counterparts in the suburbs. However, the AIOs and lifestyle of those families is very similar to households in their neighborhood and essentially dissimilar to their demographic cousins in the suburbs. It would be more appropriate to market to them in a manner similar to that for their neighbors.

In the suburbs, there's a nice neighborhood of million-dollar homes, residences for upper middle class traditional families with school-age children. Average household income is $250,000. Racial mix in the neighborhood is approximately 80% white, 10% African-American, and 10% all other. Just as in the prior example, African-American families in this neighborhood would be similar to their neighbors and dissimilar to a purely demographic profile. In fact, these families and their neighbors would tend to consider race irrelevant. Media messages directed to "African-Americans" would not be as effective in addressing *these* African-American households as would messages directed to successful professional people, race-unspecific.

Today's successful marketers segment by AIOs, lifestyle, and geodemographics. Emerging technology presents an opportunity to take that segmentation approach to a whole new level.

Split Cable

Today most of America is wired with cable and there are over a hundred channel choices. That number may soon surpass five hundred, to include such specialties as The Geranium Channel, devoted exclusively to the growing of, what else, geraniums. The implications are enormous, as the technology exists to split the commercial messages on hundreds of channels in thousands of geodemographics.

You've probably noted that at 28 and 58 past the hours channels break to local commercial messages. Billy Bob's Car City and Martha Mae's Furniture Warehouse are major players here in town but fifty miles from here no one's ever heard of them. They'd like to run TV advertising but only on a local basis. No problem. Every hour, there are four minutes in which the local cable company can run whatever it wants, covering only the local market area. Now, though, the local cable company has the ability to split a local segment into as many sub-segments as it wishes. Cable companies are already doing this in many other major markets and it's just a matter of time before it's the norm everywhere. With this technology a Polish delicatessen, previously not a qualified prospect for television advertising, can run spots carried only in its ten-square-block marketing area. Sure, cost per cable household is high but the total cost is affordable and their message reaches a very high proportion of their target market.

Larger organizations can utilize split cable to target different geo-demographics with different messages on different channels. There is every reason to consider such a strategy as an alternative to a one-size-fits-all national ad campaign and marketers can test market the concept in local markets as cable companies expand capabilities for split cable advertising.

Extrinsic Segmentation Profiles
Let's take a look at six persons who represent market segments based on AIOs, lifestyle extrinsics.

Clark Sheffield is 15, a ninth-grader at the high school. He's a good kid, makes good grades, but, like most of his generation, is very different from his parents. His primary interests are girls, video games, rap music, action movies, and extreme sports. His folks have tried to discourage him from skateboarding down the barn roof to no avail. Clark does not read books or magazines, watches only wrestling and extreme sports on TV, and uses the Internet as his primary media outlet. He has no awareness or opinions about politics or world events.

Clark earns about $50 a week doing yard work in the neighborhood, and spends most of it at the mall where he hangs out. His major purchases are movies, pizza, T-shirts, and the baggy pants he wears halfway down his cheeks. Opinion leaders are rap stars and major skateboarders, chosen at least in part because his parents can't stand them. He drinks Pepsi because he likes the babes in their commercials and his parents prefer Coke.

Grace Byron is 25, college-educated, and associate director of the local Center for Women. She is very active in numerous community organizations supporting women, the underprivileged, and the environment. She subscribes to four special interest publications and the two more liberal national newsmagazines. Grace reads about ten books a year, primarily those of leading feminist authors, and watches TV an average of twelve hours a week, primarily Animal Planet and talk shows either led by women or on which women are serious contributors.

Grace has a salary of $28,000 a year, which she spends mostly on food, shelter, functional clothing, and other necessities. Before making a purchase she investigates the provider's record for workers' rights and the environment. She responds very positively to media messages in which women are portrayed properly. By contrast, she totally tunes out messages featuring good ol' boys or pompous businessmen and is infuriated by messages that patronize women or present women as trivial, scatterbrained second-class citizens.

Addison Waveland, 35, dropped out of high school at sixteen to support his mother and three younger siblings. Over the years he has built a successful small contracting business, which currently employs three full-time helpers. He has no involvement with the downtown business community and organizations but has established strategic alliances with the large contractors in the area who know they can always rely on Addison to handle an outsourced project. Addison subscribes to the local paper, mostly for the sports section, and to magazines dedicated to deer hunting and bass fishing. All day he listens to sports talk radio and manages to find TV programming about football twelve months a year. He has a basic distrust of politicians who talk about helping people who never had a chance since no one ever did anything for him and he made it on his own. Addison is proud to be an American and considers himself the fulfillment of the American Dream.

Addison clears about $80,000 a year from his business and has a real nice house, most of which he built himself. His discretionary income goes mostly into hunting, fishing, and a stock car he's working on. Addison is one of those folks who responds to traditional American values and he wants to do business with people and firms who think the way he does. He's not averse to paying top dollar for something of the highest quality—he just dropped almost three grand on a lawn tractor—but you'll totally turn him off with an appeal to impress others with the latest style and the "right" labels. Addison figures there's something fundamentally wrong with a person who would spend a hundred dollars on a polo shirt so he could impress people with its label.

Cornelia Freeport is 45, a housewife with four children, age 10 to 18. She is married to an economist who earns $29,000 a year. Cornelia feels very strongly about traditional family values and is an active member of her church, where she conducts religious studies with six-to-eight-year-olds on Wednesday nights and Sunday mornings. Her only other group affiliation is with an organization of mothers that acts as a watchdog over the school system and its curriculum. She is a regular viewer of daytime television and spends most evenings watching network sitcoms and reality shows. Her opinion leaders are conservative religious leaders and politicians who take strong stands against moral relativism and permissiveness.

Cornelia has a limited budget, spent mostly on food and household essentials. She is very aware of ingredients and product quality in everything she buys but is even more concerned about supporting companies that stand for traditional values. She boycotts companies that sponsor anything other than wholesome family entertainment or that extend employees benefits packages beyond traditional married couples. Cornelia and her friends maintain and regularly update a list of companies whose products they will and will not buy.

Roscoe Halsted, 55, made a bunch of money in the stock market bubble and got out at just the right time. He has a net worth in the mid-seven figures and wants to be sure everyone knows about it. Roscoe paid over ten grand for his watch, which he'll push within a foot of your face if you don't compliment him about it within five minutes of meeting him. He pays more than a hundred dollars for the bottle of wine he has with dinner each evening, mainly because it's the most expensive brand on the market. Roscoe is divorced but does not lack for companionship interested in helping him spend his dividend checks. Folks inviting him over for dinner have learned to take an empty bottle of his favorite wine, fill it with five-dollar-a-gallon private label product winos speak highly of, and he never knows the difference. Roscoe's opinion leaders include anyone who has more money than he does and his primary reference group is the rich and famous who take thirty-day luxury cruises and spend summers on the Riviera.

As you may have surmised, Roscoe is a somewhat insecure person whose extrinsics focus on anything that makes him feel important, exclusive, and young. He's a big favorite, and a big tipper, at the Gulf Breeze Gentleman's Club. Roscoe's doctor has warned him he's headed for trouble but he's simply told the doc "No problem. Price is no object."

Roscoe's TV watching is limited to cable business channels and political talk shows. He reads neither books nor magazines, but will occasionally pick up USA Today and peruse the business sections. Most evenings he hires a limo to take him out clubbing or he stays home and watches pay-per-view movies.

In many ways Roscoe presents a dilemma to marketers, who can feel a bit sorry for him as they take his money. However, in a free economy, dedicated to satisfying the customer, there will always be an opportunity to help people pay premium prices just so they can say they did.

Reta Kenmore is 65 and quite a contrast to Roscoe. Thanks to forty years of savvy real estate investments she's worth about twice Roscoe's net worth but you might never know it. Reta understands the meaning of class and quality and will accept nothing less than the finest but is disinterested in showing off. Her wardrobe is best described as understated elegance that conveys an impression of quality material and workmanship. Everything in her home is of the highest quality and invites a closer inspection to reveal all the minute details of craftsmanship.

Reta's standards are uncompromising. She does business only with those who are best at what they do and are of the highest integrity. She expects service and follow-up and is glad to pay for it.

Reta actively supports the arts and has endowed programs to help talented young people go to schools specializing in theater and art. She is an avid reader of literature and publications dedicated to art and design. Her TV viewing is limited, predominantly Public Broadcasting, where she is well aware of firms underwriting quality programming.

Summing Up

Hopefully, these sample profiles gave you an insight to the process of describing market segments according to AIOs, lifestyle, and extrinsics. Perhaps one or more described examples of segments your firm is interested in. Now it's time to put all the pieces together in the marketing plan.

Chapter 7

The Marketing Plan

The first six chapters were the foundation. We now understand what marketing is, the nature of a marketing orientation, and the role of marketing in the organization. We have an awareness of the external environment, the process of gathering information, and points concerning market segmentation. With that in place we're ready to do the marketing plan.

Framework for Planning

Effective strategic planning goes beyond an assessment of today and seeks to envision the world of tomorrow. Start with current trends and ask yourself whether it is reasonable to expect them to continue. Long-term trends, such as the increasing proportion of meals consumed outside the home or decreasing sales of VCRs, are likely to continue. Short-term fads, such as coonskin hats and low-carb diets, are more likely to be disappointing in the out years. It may be reasonable to make a major capital investment to address a long-term trend. However, management might choose short-term promotions and advertising themes to exploit short-term opportunities.

As you envision the future, consider ways in which you can cause change, not just react to it. Do this with an eye to the most likely competitive response and its consequences. Realize that projecting the future is educated guesswork at best and consider what your options would be if the future world turns out to be very different from today's best guesses. Build in flexibility as you match the organization and resources with evolving opportunities in the marketplace.

A marketing plan includes both strategy and tactics. Strategy is the big picture, describing the ultimate objectives of the plan in terms of measurable results in a specific time frame. Tactics are the operational activities employed to achieve the strategy. So, strategy is the invasion of Europe by establishing a beachhead at Normandy. A tactic would be for a platoon to take out a machine gun emplacement covering a landing site.

Let me reiterate an earlier point about the need to integrate strategy and tactics, contrary to the traditional approach of first devising a strategy and then considering implementation. Strategy should be developed with an awareness of tactical capabilities and tactical advantages should be a major consideration in the development of a strategy.

Steps of the Marketing Plan

Step 1: Define the Business Mission

I've already discussed the need to define the business you're in. This step must already be in place before embarking on the strategic planning process. Therefore, for the remainder of this chapter, I will approach the steps of the marketing plan from the perspective of a stand-alone strategic business unit (SBU) operating as a profit center that has defined its business mission in terms of customer needs, not products presently produced. For a smaller company the SBU could be tantamount to the organization as a whole.

Step 2: Situation Analysis

In the business world the situation analysis is often referred to with the acronym SWOT (Strengths/Weaknesses/Opportunities/Threats). Take your time with this step and don't cut corners as you assess yourself, the competition, and the external environment today and as you envision it in the future.

Strengths are what you do well relative to competitive alternatives. I've already described potential advantages in production and implementation. Also consider your brand awareness and reputation. If customers and prospects within a market perceive that your product is in some meaningful way superior you may have an opportunity to sell that value and command a premium price. You may have a brand name with a high level of positive recognition that lends itself to ancillary product introductions. For example, Harley-Davidson is more than a product, it's an aspirational reference group. You'll see their logo on clothing, beverages, and everything in between. Harley enjoys licensing revenues and, even more important, advertising exposure they don't even have to pay for. Sports franchises play the same game, licensing top-end attire that's in high demand among young fans who also view the telecasts and attend games in person to cheer on their opinion leaders.

A brand with a good reputation in a narrowly-defined market may present an opportunity to exploit its name in new product lines or line extensions. Dole, highly respected in pineapple, extends its quality image to other fresh and canned fruits, immediately achieving consumer acceptance. Budweiser discovered that the most effective strategy for attacking the light beer category was to line-extend with Bud Light. Potential advantages of extending brand names can have the pitfall of diminishing the unique positioning of the flagship brand, however, a point I'll address in detail in the next chapter.

Weaknesses, no surprise, are the flip side of strengths—those areas in which you do not compare favorably. These do not necessarily imply insurmountable obstacles but may simply point the way to more viable alternatives. An airline relatively weak in the coast-to-coast segment of the market might decide to concentrate expansion among short-haul regional markets. A food company with a low share in the condensed soup market might shift its attention to the premium ready-to-eat segment in microwaveable packaging.

On the other hand weaknesses that represent vulnerability to competitive attack may need to be defended with some combination of new product introductions or promotions. At some point, however, weak segments of a business must be abandoned if they cannot sustain profitability. For management this can be challenging indeed, pursuing strengths while either defending or eliminating areas of weakness. Just as in war, rapidly shifting conditions in the external environment can favor one organization and devastate another less adaptable organization. The Nazis were having great success in their invasion of the Soviet Union until winter set in. IBM was king of the hill with mainframes until the personal computer came along. And

Kodak was synonymous with photography until the digital camera was invented. You can't control the weather but if your SWOT analysis identifies a weakness in leadership of emerging technology, that's probably something to be addressed before it becomes a crisis. There won't be much of a point running a promotion for film when everyone's taking digital pictures.

Opportunities are those courses of action suggested by strengths relative to competitive alternatives. **Threats**, taking the view that the glass is half full, are opportunities to address deficiencies or defend your turf.

A SWOT analysis is not some quick-and-dirty pushover you knock out in half a day. Much of it is dynamic, updated by your Decision Support System (DSS) on a regular basis. But some issues will need to be addressed with marketing research to quantify and prioritize the SWOTs. As you formalize the strategic planning process decide when everything must be completed and back up the calendar to set deadlines for each step of the process. For instance, let's say you're developing products for the holiday season, to be in stores by October 31. You will need to call on the trade in July, so all product and promotion details must be finalized by June 30. To complete product/promotion work by then the SWOT analysis must be completed by April 30. Thus, by January 31 you must make final decisions concerning primary research activities to be conducted. So, just after verifying that all this year's products and promotions are on the shelves and all the details have been implemented at outlet level, it's time to get started for next year. Properly done the strategic planning process is an ongoing loop.

Step 3: Set Objectives

With all necessary information on hand and the SWOT analysis complete it's time to set objectives to address priorities designed to fulfill the organization's mission. These must not be vague and general like "Achieve category leadership in the gourmet cat food market," but very specific: "Achieve a 30% share of the single-serving gourmet cat food market within six months of campaign launch." Specific objectives and marketing strategies will be developed to address existing and new products among existing and new customers. Let's take a look at alternative marketing strategies in detail.

Market Penetration: Existing Product to Existing Market

In many situations selling an existing product to its current customers is the foundation of your business. Often there's no better place to look for increasing sales than among those present satisfied customers. The question is: Can you persuade them to use more of it more often?

For years consumer products companies have addressed market penetration for discretionary products with large single-serving sizes and packouts. Instead of a 12-ounce can the standard has become a 24-ounce bottle. Instead of a 6-pack, sell them a two-by-six refrigerator pack that increases in-home inventory of cold product.

Increase usage occasions! Orange juice is not just for breakfast anymore, have a second glass in the middle of the afternoon. Our ranch dressing also makes a great party dip.

With the 80–20 rule in mind, encourage heavy users to increase their consumption even more through promotion. Such a strategy could be implemented with coupons, most of which will be redeemed by current users, or premiums such as a cookbook featuring recipes with your product, free with four proofs of purchase. Then, with the cookbook, and afterwards, do a little one-on-one marketing with a steady flow of coupons.

Many organizations approach market penetration with frequent user promotions. "Stay three nights and get a weekend for free." "Accumulate a certain number of miles and get a free flight, plus we'll upgrade you to business class."

Technology makes it easier to follow up with existing customers, a slam dunk if they made their purchase on line. Amazon regularly e-mails suggestions about books I might be interested in and I often make a purchase on the spot. If I buy a ticket to see a ball game I expect to hear from those folks the next season by the day single-game tickets go on sale.

Some of the glamorous nightclubs in town have a fifty-cent cover charge, but for five bucks they'll sell you a pass good for a year. If you currently drop by once a month, let's try to get you in here once a week.

Market penetration goes back to the concept of the lifetime customer and how it's more viable to satisfy and maintain your current customer base than create new customers. The longer you're in business, the more important market penetration should be.

Product Development: New Product to Existing Market

A logical extension to market penetration—existing products to existing markets—is product development, selling new products to your present satisfied customers. You know who these customers are and where they live, the features and benefits most important to them, their attitudes/interests/opinions (AIOs), other lifestyle characteristics, and extrinsics important to them. Thus, it's fairly straightforward to determine related and ancillary products that would be of interest to them and to develop advertising and promotional messages that will appeal to them.

If you're buying my car wax, I'll bet you'd be a good prospect for my engine degreaser and wheel cleaner. If you just spent twenty bucks for a team T-shirt, you might be interested in a jacket for a hundred. If you're having a burger and fries, you might want to top it off with a hot apple pie.

I had noted how companies or brands with a solid reputation might consider new products that would be recognized and tried by satisfied customers or persons interested in affiliating with the brand. Nike has also done this in a direct manner by targeting fitness watches to persons using their running shoes.

Look at your current customers and think about new products you might be able to sell them, especially if your present business relationship offers a competitive advantage. A classic example of this is Internet services offered by cable companies and phone companies, who are already wired into your home. If it's not feasible for your organization to address these opportunities directly, consider establishing a strategic alliance and partnership.

Market Development: Existing Product to New Market

Generally, we think of market development as the expansion into new geographic areas. A regional brand goes national, or a domestic marketer moves into new global markets. The cheese steak restaurant chain in Philly opens outlets in New York, McDonald's enters China and Viet Nam.

However, market development might also focus on new *customers* within existing markets. Consider, for example, the dishwasher detergent market. This is a non-discretionary product immune to market penetration. No one is going to come along with a new brand people love so much that they do the dishes twice as often. The product category will grow at a slow, highly predictable rate, with a cause-and-effect relationship to the number of dishwashers in active use. Any sales gain above that of the total category will come as a result of an increased market share of the category, at the expense of competitive alternatives.

Gaining share within a category by promoting brand-switching— taking customers away from the competition—does not fit the academic definition of "market development" because, technically, all those customers comprise the one market. However, in the real world "new customers" are tantamount to "new markets" and marketing managers should always include tactics for attacking the competition's customer base within their strategic plan.

A strategy of market development by attracting new customers in an existing market is particularly important in services, especially those featuring close one-on-one relationships. Think about the residential real estate market in your community. A firm aspiring to increase its share of the market will do so by prospecting and closing relationships with buyers and sellers who would otherwise have done business with a competitive agency or sold their home themselves. Similarly, a specialty outsourcer is likewise fighting against its competition for market share but also has the opportunity to increase the size of the total pie by creating business relationships with clients who previously performed their functions in-house.

Diversification: New Product to New Market

Approach diversification with the greatest of care. As Harvey Mackay warns us: "When a person with money meets a person with experience, the person with the experience winds up with the money and the person with the money winds up with the experience" (*Swim with the Sharks without being Eaten Alive* [1988], New York: Fawcett Columbine, p.132).

There are circumstances where diversification involves little risk such as the example of Harley-Davidson licensing its name for items of clothing. No capital investment was required on their part and although clothing represented a new market it was targeted to their present aspirational reference group. By contrast, you face considerable risk embarking on the marketing of products and services with which you are unfamiliar, especially if you face significant investment to get into the game. Think everything through very carefully to estimate the up-front investment needed to generate the first dollar of revenue and the time frame and additional investment expected before the venture gets into the black.

Diversification will be particularly challenging if it necessitates going into channels with which you are unfamiliar. If that's the case, not only are you attempting to enter a market you know little or nothing about, you're also facing the problem of having to establish new channel relationships to deal with issues of execution and implementation largely unknown to you.

I was dealing with a soft drink manufacturer that decided to diversify into the wine business. Their rationale seemed reasonable enough: the kids are drinking our pop, so let's have mom and dad drink our wine. They had an ad agency that handled their soft drink brands and the agency's execs could readily take on an ad campaign for a wine. So they dropped several tens of millions of dollars to buy out a wine company only to make some discoveries any of their truck drivers could have told them if they'd asked. First of all, wine was sold in many outlets in which they currently had no business. That issue was manageable. Not so was the fact that their present business was conducted with direct store delivery whereas the wine business, by law, was done through independent wholesalers with whom they had no experience. The learning curve turned out to be too steep and they were forced to abandon the venture, selling out at dimes on the dollar.

Product Portfolio Matrices

A valuable tool in brand management and strategic planning is the use of matrices comparing status, features, and positioning of the organization's brands or the firm's status within a product category. You may have noted that the prior segment, describing new and existing products in new and existing markets, was in fact a 2x2 matrix. Matrices are easy to use and a valuable tool for assessing current situations and planning for the future. Often such matrices will also include competitive brands and organizations. Let's first note one of the better-known matrices for assessing current brands, a firm's status within a product category, or the overall performance of an SBU.

The Boston Consulting Group's Growth-Share Matrix

The Boston Consulting Group (BCG) 2x2 matrix contrasts market growth rate (High/Low) with market share (also High/Low). It's been around since 1969 and one of the reasons for its staying power is that the names of entities in its four corners are catchy, descriptive, and lend themselves to strategic implications. To keep the discussion simple I'll discuss the BCG matrix in terms of individual brands or products. Similarly the matrix could be adapted to describe a firm's overall situation in a category or the organization's standing in an industry as a whole.

A product enjoying a high share in a high-growth market is a Star; a high share in a low-growth market is a Cash Cow (You've been hearing the term "cash cow" for years, now you know who made it famous.); a low share in a high-growth market is a Problem Child; and a low share in a low-growth market is a Dawg.

STAR: HIGH SHARE IN A HIGH-GROWTH MARKET. Stars are often the innovative new products in emerging markets, in many cases from new companies with a breakthrough in technology that propelled them into a leadership position. Likewise, stars may be from established firms on the cutting edge of new product development, defining themselves with a marketing orientation that re-defines the game of satisfying a segment's needs and alters the product/service landscape. An implicit marketing strategy is that firms invest in stars in hope of future profits. An ideal situation is that a star can attain profitability relatively soon after its introduction and ride the profit wave for a considerable time before competitors pose a viable threat. Unfortunately, in today's fast-changing marketplace, some stars *never* turn a profit and wind up leading the organization to ruin, many examples of which can be found among e-commerce firms. The segment was growing rapidly, but the investment required in traditional media advertising to gain awareness and trial more than devoured profits. Making it worse, the e-commerce business model was easily duplicated, enabling competitors to be up and running within days. In an attempt to gain a foothold, new players were forced to compete on price, forcing down prices and profits for the industry as a whole.

The airline and transportation industries faced similar problems in the early 1980s following deregulation. Passenger airline traffic grew, but for the major carriers—classified as stars with high share in a high-growth market—profits were hard to come by. New upstart carriers caused overall fares to decline since established carriers were forced to cut prices or lose business. In the trucking industry new companies sought entry with promotional pricing below their costs. By the time they went out of business those upstarts severely damaged profit pictures for the big guys.

In the old days having a star in your portfolio usually translated to a long period of profits, well worth an investment in the early years. Today, firms need to give a great deal of thought to the prospects of a turkey ever being able to fly.

CASH COW: HIGH SHARE IN A LOW-GROWTH MARKET. There's something to be said about being a dominant player in a mature market, namely the cash. Traditional thinking suggested that you harvest those cash cows to finance the stars that would become tomorrow's cash cows and start the cycle all over again. The ad agencies loved doing things that way, since new product introductions are their big ticket items. Today, with the high cost of introducing new products and the profit uncertainty of stars, the philosophy has evolved to have marketing managers ask why they should make steaks out of a cash cow as long as it's giving milk. Hold onto them as long as possible and do just enough merchandising and promotion to retain the core groups of loyal users.

A low-growth market is unlikely to draw new entries positioned against an entrenched leader, a noteworthy advantage for long-term profits. New players in a mature market will usually seek out a niche rather than taking on the leader head-to-head.

Something I've always found intriguing about the BCG matrix is that it considers only "high" and "low" growth markets and does not mention negative-growth markets. If an overall segment is in decline it may not remain viable for long, particularly if it is declining at a rapid rate. And when the segment dies there are no steaks left to harvest, only bones and hooves. Back when I still had the typewriter, there was one firm in town that did repairs. They set premium prices for the work, did a fair amount of business in a segment no one else was inclined to enter, and milked the cow for years. Finally, though, the segment got to the point it was no longer worth messing with and they dropped out and directed those efforts elsewhere.

Never forget that the long-term objective for any brand or any SBU is to maximize profits over its lifetime. In today's business environment, profitability of stars is uncertain. An ideal situation may be to have a ranch with as many cash cows as possible. Take good care of those cash cows, extend their lives as long as you can, and, when the time is right, harvest whatever you can.

PROBLEM CHILD: LOW SHARE IN A HIGH-GROWTH MARKET. Problem Children are also called "Question Marks" but the respective names refer to entirely different strategic situations. The classic designation "Problem Child" applies to a brand that is a long-term unsuccessful player in a high-growth market, an untenable state. Managers finding themselves the not-so-proud parents of problem children face the unpleasant task of determining reasons for failure and ascertaining whether the brand will ever be a viable entry in the segment. The implicit strategy for a problem child is "Double or Quit" but don't use "double" as a universal standard. For instance, management might determine that an existing brand, with a 5% share of market, must reach a 10% share level, or a 20% level, or even a 50% level to be viable and if that is not attainable the brand should be dropped. Unfortunately, marketing managers, especially the brand manager him or herself, are so emotionally attached to a product they just can't say goodbye. But as parents of 28-year-olds still living at home can tell you, there comes a time to stop supporting the problem child and, with love, kick him out the door.

A "Question Mark" is also a brand with a low share in a high-growth market, but its distinguishing characteristic is that it's only been around for a short while. By definition, you have a zero share of market when you enter an established product category and the only way you can go lower than that is to have product returns exceed product sales. Early in its sales history your new product is literally a question mark: You don't know whether it will soar into category leadership and become a star or become mired down as an also-ran problem child. The one thing that is certain, however, is that it won't remain a question mark for long. At some pre-determined point, by some objective standard, you're going to have to call it what it is and take whatever steps are necessary.

DAWG: LOW SHARE IN A LOW-GROWTH MARKET. It's one thing being the dominant player in a low-growth or even a negative-growth market: You can milk the cow till it runs dry. It's something else being an also-ran in such a segment. The dawg is never going to hunt and there's only one thing to do with it: Shoot it between the eyes and turn your people and resources elsewhere.

The General Electric Strategic Planning Grid
The GE grid, instead of evaluating current products, is a tool for determining whether a firm should consider investing in a particular industry or product category. It's a 3x3 matrix, with designations of high, medium, and low. in contrast to the 2x2 high and low configuration of the BCG matrix, and evaluates the attractiveness of a proposed activity as contrasted with the organization's relative strength for addressing the activity.

If both activity attractiveness and organization strength are rated high, or if one is rated high and the other medium, the activity is color-coded green and it is considered a good candidate for a successful entry. By contrast, two "lows" or one low/one medium are color-coded red, not viable. Everything else, including the two high/low combinations or a medium/medium, is yellow and a maybe.

The BCG and GE matrices, and others like them, are valuable but limited tools for strategic planning. BCG only addresses existing products and GE only addresses existing industries, neither of which will be useful for identifying and exploiting new breakthrough opportunities. However, they get you off to a good start in the planning process, helping you survey your current product portfolio, your organization's capabilities, and the external environment.

Step 4: Develop the Marketing Strategy
Just a few top-line comments on this step, which I'll discuss in detail in the final six chapters of this book. The marketing strategy is an action plan that identifies target markets and how they will be addressed with the marketing mix, the four Ps (Product/Place/Promotion/Price). It describes tactics that will be employed and outlines points of execution, implementation, and follow-up.

It's important to note that Step 3 of the marketing plan: Set Objectives, and Step 4: Develop the Marketing Strategy, are not isolated discrete events. As managers set strategic objectives they already have an idea of products that will be in the mix and target markets that will be addressed. They will have identified points of differential advantage, assessed competitive alternatives, and uncovered target market segments with unmet needs. So, by the time they finalize the strategic objective of achieving a 30% share of the single-serving gourmet cat food market, management already knows the products to be offered and market segments to be targeted. Just as tactical advantages affect the marketing strategy, so does the marketing strategy influence the overall objectives. All of this is consistent with an approach of a marketing plan built from the bottom up, not dictated from the top down. Throughout this very fluid process, managers continuously assess marketing opportunities in light of the mission and capabilities of the organization and the risk/reward of particular market segments.

One of the most difficult challenges in developing a marketing plan is determining market segments that will *not* be targeted. Then, for those that will be addressed, the next major decision is to determine how many market segments there will be. Every additional target segment adds to marketing expenditures. The key question, difficult to answer with a high degree of certainty, is whether there's a payoff for those investments. If multiple segments can be addressed with the same product, in different media, cost implications are far less than a situation in which a segment would necessitate a separate product.

Just as in sports or war the marketing plan must be drafted with an eye to the competition. A certain target market might have limited potential for your organization but would you wish to leave it uncontested, easy plucking for competitors? And would that uncontested business enable the competition to get a foot in the door, better able to oppose you in other areas? Likewise, a segment might not offer profit potential for you but could force a competitive response costly to them and which would also divert their resources. Guerilla attacks that cost you thousands might be a good investment if they prompt a massive response costing them millions of dollars and hundreds of man-hours.

CHAPTER 8

The Nature of Products and Services

Generally, we think of products as tangibles and services as intangibles, but both products and services are a combination of tangibles *and* intangibles. So, let's define Product, the first of the four Ps, as everything—tangibles, intangibles, and extrinsics—that a customer receives in the exchange. A quarter century ago, Theodore Levitt advised marketers to emphasize intangibles when marketing physical products and to tangibilize services ("Marketing Intangible Products and Product Intangibles," *Harvard Business Review.* May/June, 1981). For a physical product, intangibles are the extrinsics such as prestige, love, and affiliation. As I described earlier, a product's features must be compatible with the needs of the target market but extrinsics are the sizzle that sells the steak. You don't sell a car, you sell prestige. You don't sell brown pop in a bottle, you sell youth and affiliation. Do the same thing with services. Sell the benefits of success, peace-of-mind, fewer hassles, whatever, but with one further consideration: since services cannot be touched, felt, smelled, or stored, find a way to tangibilize the intangibles to make them seem more real. To achieve this many organizations that market services adopt an appropriate tangible symbol: Prudential's rock, Allstate's good hands, Travelers' umbrella. Additionally, firms may adopt high standards for employee attire, a strategy made famous by IBM, whose employees were known for the professional appearance and impression they always brought with them. Today, many real estate franchises insist on an employee uniform to create a tangible impression of consistent quality. Consider as well the attire of employees in businesses ranging from law firms to the finer hotels. Additionally, all types of firms may benefit from high quality physical facilities: inside their doors, the building itself, and the cleanliness and landscaping of their grounds.

The baseline for products and services is the core offering, the bare bones minimum product with no special features, an undifferentiated commodity sold on price. Marketers augment the core offering with supplemental features important to the target market, creating value for which customers will pay more. As we've already seen, marketing is all about the creation of value.

Standardization and quality control enhance value for both products and services. This is a particularly important concern for services, where wide variations in the performance of individual service providers can result in inconsistent quality and customer satisfaction. For example, you may be very happy with the haircut you get at a national chain in your community but chances are you wouldn't be as thrilled with what you'd get from the first available barber at the same chain in a location halfway across the country. Thus, since customer loyalty, recognition, and value are often a function of consistency, high-end service providers go to great lengths to hire the right personnel, invest in training, and standardize their procedures. No matter where you go you know what to expect and you know it will be done right at a Marriott. That's value worth paying for compared to the core product down the street at less than half the price.

Another unique aspect of services is perishability. That is, if there's no buyer when the service is ready to be performed, it's gone forever. When the plane takes off with an empty seat, when an apartment or motel room is vacant, or when a lawyer sits in his office playing solitaire, that revenue is gone for good. Therefore, service providers are likely to have differential pricing: Rooms are cheap in New Orleans the week after Mardi Gras and you can get some great fares to London in March.

Some Points About Products

Here are some of the descriptive terms concerning the array of products an organization markets:

A **product item** is a specific version of a particular product or service. In the trade, it's known as a stock-keeping unit (SKU) which is identified by its own unique universal product code (UPC), the bar-code read by a scanner at the checkout. For Schick, the Quattro razor, the four-count blade refill, and the eight-count blade refill are three SKUs under the brand name Quattro. Similarly, the eight-ounce bottle, sixteen-ounce bottle, and twenty-four ounce bottle are three SKUs of Thousand Island salad dressing marketed by Kraft for their Light Done Right brand.

A **product line** is a group of closely-related product items. For Schick one of those would be their line of razors, and for Kraft it would be their line of salad dressings.

The **product mix** is the composite list of all the organization's offerings, every product item they sell.

The **width of the product mix** is the total number of product lines an organization markets. Kraft has a line of salad dressings, a line of barbecue sauce, a line of cheeses, etc.

The **depth of the product line** is the number of product items in a given product line. It's important to note, however, that marketers often use the term depth to refer to the number of distinct brands in a particular line, not the number of product items.

A fundamental priority early in the strategic planning process is assessment of product items and product lines and a comparison of these with those of the competition. Managers can start thinking about existing and new markets with an eye on uniqueness, gaps, and opportunities.

Product Classifications

Products are classified according to the amount of effort generally expended in shopping for them. However, a product's classification may not be consistent for all persons in all situations and many opportunities are to be found by stepping outside the classifications.

Convenience Products
We most often think of convenience products as being relatively inexpensive, routinely purchased, and requiring a minimum of shopping

effort. You tank up the car, go into the store to pay, and without even thinking about it, grab a can of pop on ice at the checkout, and you're on your way. No big deal. Or is it?

Even though very little thought and effort went into the decision to buy that can of pop many important marketing activities preceded the purchase. A lifetime of advertising exposure and buying behavior may have created awareness, usage, and brand loyalty, all of which came into play at the moment you saw those cans on ice. Or, for whatever reason, you may have tried a new product, one you'd heard about but didn't remember until there it was. But the key point is that some sales rep made a call on the trade to sell that display and someone else built it and stocked it.

Let's consider a related situation. For ten years you've started off every morning with the same brand of cereal. Each week you walk through the cereal aisle and buy a box without even looking at the price. That is, until today, when the product was sold out except for one box that had been bashed. Then, looking at the empty shelves, you're stuck by how dirty they are. So ends ten years of brand loyalty.

Every marketer dreams of building a core group of loyal users who don't even have to think about their purchase decision. Just be sure your product is there and properly presented when they're ready to buy. Once they start to think about something that used to be automatic, you lose.

Though I've started with examples of the usual relatively inconsequential decisions we think of as convenience products, there are other very different situations in which a significant purchase could be classified as a convenience product because of time utility. If I need something now and you have it now, I may see it as a convenience product for which I'll pay a premium price. Let's say you're in a foreign county undergoing revolution and anarchy. You've fled to the airport seeking escape and at the ticket counter the agent tells you they have one seat left today. It's in First Class and has a one-way fare of $4000. Chances are pretty good that you'll take the seat rather than spend the night at the airport in hope something cheaper might come up tomorrow.

In a couple of weeks I'm going out of town. I have to catch lunch, check into a motel, and get into the city on a Sunday afternoon. I know where I'm eating lunch. I pull out the brochure for my motel chain of choice and discover that they have locations only on the other side of town from my restaurant. So, I check the brochure for my second choice and son of a gun they have a location on the very same street as my lunch location. Their rate is about twenty bucks more than I want to pay but I don't care. It's convenient.

Olive runs an office supply store in the mall. I know darned well there are better prices to be had at the office supply superstore but folks still deal with Olive because it's pleasant and easy, she delivers, and she'll even stock your supply cabinet for you.

Whatever you market, you may be able to command a premium price simply by being at the proper place at the proper time. Save customers time and effort and help them get their concerns out of the way and done with. That's value worth paying for.

Shopping Products
Shopping products generally require some, though not extensive, comparison shopping unless they're convenience products. Yes, that statement sounds confusing and requires explanation.

Tires could be an example of a shopping product. You might compare different brands and different product items within a line. Additionally, you might compare competitive stores to check prices, meet their people, and get an impression of their physical facilities. Finally, after investing a few hours over a few days, you decide what to buy from whom, a classic example of buying behavior for a shopping product.

But let's consider an alternative situation: you have a blowout while driving I-70 near Goodland, Kansas. The tire store there has an acceptable brand, but not the one you're loyal to. However, it will take a full day to truck a tire of your favorite brand in from Denver. You don't feel like waiting around so you take what's there, making the tire a convenience good. This is just another example of why marketers must not define their products with rigid classifications.

Shopping products are subdivided into homogeneous and heterogeneous shopping products. This has nothing to do with what they do with each other on the shelves after the lights go out, but with the perceived differences among competitive offerings. **Homogeneous shopping products** are considered undifferentiated among brands and so, for comparable product features, are bought mostly on price. Examples often cited are washers, dryers, and TV sets.

If you've been paying any attention whatsoever, a big red light should have just gone on in your head. Remember: Anything can be and must be differentiated. Classifying your products as homogeneous shopping products probably says a lot more about you (You're a lousy marketer.) than it does about the product class. Just consider washers and dryers. Maytag has established the reputation of a superior product that can command a premium price. Sears not only differentiates Kenmore by the quality product, but also by the store itself and its service after the sale.

Some products truly are undifferentiated commodities. When I go to the home improvement store to buy lumber I don't know or care who the manufacturer is. Furthermore, it's highly unlikely that the home improvement store carries more than one line of treated pine two-by-fours. For me the lumber is a shopping product involving a relatively quick decision of where to go to make the purchase. However, this does not imply that marketers cannot differentiate themselves when calling on home improvement store headquarters. Unless a manufacturer can demonstrate superior value of some kind, their products will not attain availability in the retail outlet. They can create that value by undercutting the competitors' prices, not healthy for the bottom line, or differentiate themselves in how they do business. But one way or another, either for the ultimate consumer or within trade channels, the product or the vendor can and must be differentiated on some basis or be forced to compete solely on price. For you as a marketer, nothing should be classified as a homogeneous shopping product. **Heterogeneous shopping products,** a term that should be synonymous with "shopping products" for competent marketers, refers to shopping products with identifiable product differentiation that could include intrinsic features and quality or extrinsics such as prestige and affiliation. Examples of heterogeneous shopping products commonly sighted are furniture, clothing, and cruise lines.

For all shopping products marketers must assess existing and potential points of differentiation and how those points can address needs of target market segments or channel members. Points that offer some competitive advantage that is not readily duplicated will be a focus of your strategic plan.

Specialty products are those for which a customer is brand loyal, will accept no substitutes, and will go out of their way to seek. Generally we think of these as being at the high end of a product class: Rolls-Royce, Rolex, or Waterford. However, once again, marketers should not restrict their thinking to rigid classifications. Just as a shopping good can be a convenience product, depending on the buying situation, so can a shopping good—or even a convenience product—be a specialty product for a core group of users. Men's slacks are considered shopping products by most people, but not by me. For almost forty years, the only jeans I've worn are shrink-to-fit button-fly Levi's. I can't get them in the east any more, so buy them online from a retailer in Colorado. Ketchup is usually thought of as a convenience product but I can't ever remember buying anything other than Heinz. There's a lesson for marketers: *Any* product can become a specialty good with the development of loyal users who will accept no substitute. That loyalty, known as the consumer franchise, is the goodwill on your balance sheet that translates to profitable customers.

Finally, **unsought products** are those which potential customers are not aware of or not actively seeking. Until, that is, a proactive marketer makes them aware, makes them seek, or, at the least has a dominant presence when the need arises. An example of the latter situation is having a full-page ad under "Plumbers" in the Yellow Pages.

A traditional *unsought* product can become *sought* through a sales force. You weren't even thinking about more insurance until speaking with an agent at a networking event. You hadn't even considered footing the bill for your own burial plot until the launching of a tasteful media campaign imploring you to spare your loved ones the burden of all those details at the time of need.

You will market unsought products as heterogeneous shopping goods, or specialty products, certainly not as convenience goods. When prospects become aware of a need it will be satisfied as something special, not as a commodity. That burial plot should really look nice. The real estate agent or insurance agent—tangible symbols of an undifferentiated service—must come across as competent and a person you'd like to do business with.

Some Basics About Branding

As I did with products, here are some descriptive terms concerning the branding of those products:

A **brand** is a combination of names, terms, designs or symbols that identify a product and distinguish it from competitive offerings. The entity of a brand has two parts: the **brand name**, words that can be spoken, such as "Cadillac" (the car, the dog food, or the ranch), and the **brand mark**, elements of the brand that cannot be spoken, such as the Nike swoosh or the Mercedes star.

A **logo** is a distinctive company symbol or trademark. Examples would include the offset "E" for Dell computers, the red and white target symbol for Target, or brand-identifiable symbols for sports teams.

A **trademark** is a legally protected brand name, brand mark, logo, or phrase. I can launch any product with the name Cadillac, because "Cadillac" is a **generic product name**, a common name, which may have once had trademark protection but is now in the public domain. However, I may not use the Cadillac script and crest, which have trademark protection. I cannot call another product a "Chevrolet," as that name is not in the public domain and may only be used by General Motors Corporation. Trademarked phrases include many with which you're familiar ("Good to the last drop" for Maxwell House) and some that would seem unlikely to have trademark protection but do ("Now you're living" for Cox Cable).

Organizations fight to maintain the reputation of their brands and the integrity of their trademarks, particularly if there is a threat of them going into the public domain. Ever gone to Hamburger City and asked for a triple cheeseburger, fries, and a Coke, only to be told "We don't have Coke. Is a Pepsi OK?" That happens because The Coca-Cola Company does not want "coke" to go into the public domain meaning any brand of brown cola pop. Similarly, Xerox wants to be certain that a "Xerox copy" does not come to mean a copy run off any old brand of copier.

Name and Product Positioning

Early in the strategic planning process, it is essential to evaluate the names and implications of existing brands and your organization itself. A company named General Electric or 3M, not directly associated with a narrow product class, can readily place their corporate name on a new product for a new market. However, Xerox, a name synonymous with copiers, had difficulty placing their corporate name on other office products. To their potential clients Xerox was the copier company and not the total office solution. On a smaller scale, a business called "Just Windows" will encounter problems extending its business into heating and air conditioning contracting. Shoe City, likewise, cannot just change its name to "Shoe City and More" as it markets lines of clothing since the customer's mind perceives Shoe City to be a place to get shoes but not clothes.

Just as some corporate names like Xerox are synonymous with a product class so are some individual brands **master brands**. When you hear aspirin you think Bayer, as when you hear bleach you think Clorox, even though those are both generic products, indistinguishable from the competition. An advantage of such a situation is value and brand loyalty from the name's strong positioning, translating to profitable sales over lower-priced alternatives. A potential disadvantage is that the name may not translate well to a different product class and, furthermore, such an extension may water down the positioning of the flagship brand. Yes, you can market Clorox as powdered bleach or liquid bleach, in a variety of scents, but Clorox is bleach or at the least a product associated with cleaning. The mind might not be able to reconcile the name Clorox with cat litter and, even if such a brand were superior to competitive alternatives, it might have trouble gaining a foothold. Likewise, Bayer can have products for kids, products for adults, in a variety of forms and flavors, but Bayer is aspirin. If their company were introducing an athlete's foot treatment, an individual brand name would be more powerful than Bayer Brand Athlete's Foot

Fixer. I found it interesting when Porsche put their name on an SUV. Porsche is a sports car, not an SUV. Can "Porsche" stand as a name for family brands without undermining the position of its flagship? Should they have had a new brand name for the SUV with a notation, "Inspired by Porsche"? It may be a tough row to hoe. By contrast, consider Honda, successfully established as a leader in motorcycles and automobiles, launching ventures unto seemingly far-fetched products as generators and lawn mowers. Doesn't that also have the potential to undermine the value of the brand name Honda in its motor vehicle segments? Not at all thanks to very clever positioning of its diversifications. Honda presents its name as representing the finest quality engines instead of any one finished product. Therefore, since Honda means engines, the value of the trademarked brand can readily stand for a large number of different products targeted at numerous market segments.

It's a whole lot easier to exploit your position in the customer's mind than to try to change it. Hardee's is the burger chain favored by the guys in pick-up trucks, whereas McDonald's is the place for families and kids. Rather than try to go for the family/kid segment, Hardee's expanded its breakfast menu for product development with guys in pick-up trucks.

Wal-Mart is king of the hill in the low price mass merchandiser segment, with K-Mart a distant second. When Target made its foray into the retailing business they were careful to avoid going head-to-head against Wal-Mart but instead took the ground between Wal-Mart and moderate-priced retailers like Sears and JC Penney. Sadly for K-Mart there may no longer be a viable market position remaining for them.

Every organization must regularly assess the names and positioning for itself and its brands and determine whether there are opportunities for new strategic business units (SBUs) or new brands. Prudential means investment services, so they could extend the brand name to real estate or tax services but management might wish to consider a different brand name or create a new SBU to address an opportunity in staffing services. It is for this reason that in a merger or acquisition the acquiring organization often retains the names of the SBUs it takes over rather than replace those names with its own. The acquired SBU has a position in the mind of the customer.

In any case, a product name should mean something to the customer. Ideally, it should also say something about the product. Die Hard is a great name for a battery, Weed Eater for a string trimmer, and Aquafina for bottled water. But how about Lever 2000 for a bar of soap? Procter & Gamble is the dominant player in the product class, so Lever can't take them on head-to-head. If Lever wishes to compete other than on price, they need to find a niche market with special needs but the name Lever 2000 says nothing about either. The same is true for Dasani in the bottled water segment. It's true that water is the consummate commodity, but anything can be differentiated, if only through its name, extrinsics, and identification with a target market. But what's a Dasani and who would find it special?

You may discover that names and positioning of your firm and its brands are not what they need to be. If that's the case it may be more effective to start from scratch with new names and positions instead of what will likely be a futile attempt to reposition an existing brand or SBU. Each target market should be addressed by a product that has the features they want, with an appropriate name, promoted through a message that creates the desired image and extrinsics. The objective is to find a place in your prospect's mind and establish your product there.

Ideally, you would love to become the master brand in a category but that's unlikely to happen unless you either create or revolutionize that category. This point further supports the need to look beyond existing products, existing markets, and existing technologies. Breakthrough opportunities translate to a 100% market share for you until the competition can launch its own entry. If that time frame takes more than a few weeks or months you may have been able to rake high-profit sales off the top of the market and establish a dominant position through distribution channels and at outlet level. Even more important, your product and brand has taken a leadership position in the customer's mind. When they hear about the product they think about you. That's brand equity and means that the me-too follower will have to accept lower profit margins to have an equal likelihood of getting the sale.

On a regular basis, new technology creates new master brands in categories that find new and better ways of satisfying customer needs. Often the sudden shift completely knocks the underpinnings from a brand or an entire organization. Polaroid was once the undisputed leader in instant photography, one of the Dow 30 Industrials on the New York Stock Exchange. IBM stood alone at the top of the mainframe computer market.

There was a time when Eveready was the master brand of batteries. Until, that is, Duracell introduced the alkaline energizer and stole the "battery" position in the customer's mind. Eveready responded with the "Eveready alkaline power cell," quite a mouthful. In retrospect, the folks at Eveready realized they'd made a mistake in extending the line under the same name since "Eveready" meant old technology batteries and "Duracell" meant new technology batteries in the mind of the customer. They finally got it right, re-naming the product "Energizer" and creating a perfect and memorable symbol with the Energizer Bunny. Now it's a dog fight in the battery segment. Over time, one of those brands, through superior promotion, distribution, and merchandising, will slowly rise to share dominance and take the master brand position. The also-ran will still be viable player, though not the market leader. No one else will seriously dent the category. Ultimately, there's only room for two in the big leagues, so any another company desiring to get in the segment needs to direct its attention to developing the technology that will make the alkaline energizer obsolete, choose the right name and symbol, and instead of confronting the competition, jump right over them.

Branding Alternatives

Individual Brands

There are long-term advantages to giving each individual product its own name, its own identity, and to take a unique position in the mind of the customer. Individual branding is the philosophy of some of the leading consumer nondurable manufacturers. General Mills markets Bisquick pancake mix, Gold Medal flour, and Betty Crocker cake mixes, all products that enjoy a strong position in their respective segments. Likewise, Procter & Gamble markets coffee as Folgers, detergents as Tide and Cheer, and toothpaste as Crest. You'll see General Mills' "G" logo on cereal products, but the individual brand name is what stands out to the customer, who buys "Basic 4," not "General Mills' Basic 4." That's in contrast to Kellogg's, who employs a mix of individual brand/family brand. "Rice Krispies" is a Kellogg trademark but they nevertheless market it as "Kellogg's Rice Krispies." "Corn Flakes" and "Raisin Bran" are generic product names, so "Kellogg's Corn Flakes" and "Kellogg's Raisin Bran" are family brands, not individual brands. By contrast, "Cracklin' Oat Bran" is a pure-play individual brand featuring, in the style of General Mills, only an icon of Kellogg's corporate affiliation.

Procter & Gamble, General Mills, and Kellogg's have line-extended individual brands, always taking great care to assure that the extended product holds a position consistent with its brand name. I previously cited White Strips as consistent with the position of Crest. Similarly, "Rice Krispies Treats" are a convenient presentation of a product usage application already familiar to users.

Family Brands
Under a family branding philosophy, a number of products are marketed under the same name, usually identifying the manufacturer or retailer. Such an approach is most viable when the families of products are related with some meaningful position in the mind of the customer. I cited Honda. Also consider brands like Sony or Panasonic, family brands of consumer electronics shopping products. The name "Sony" or "Panasonic" distinguishes the brand from an unknown, unadvertised alternative. For these shopping products the brand name creates an impression of value. Little would be gained by having an individual brand name on each product line, though the manufacturer may tag on a phrase or distinctive name for some intrinsic technology.

Similarly, consider a family brand strategy for numerous lines of consumer nondurables. Kraft has taken this approach successfully with the attitude that customer satisfaction in one product line will translate to an inclination to try other product lines. You like their barbecue sauce, so you'll sample the salad dressing.

A benefit of family branding is quick recognition and acceptance. The disadvantage is that a family brand rarely, if ever, has the dominant position in a customer's mind. When you hear "cream cheese," you think "Philadelphia." Kraft would not achieve the same level of top-of-mind awareness if they named that product "Kraft Cream Cheese."

Rarely does it make sense to turn an individual brand into a family brand, especially if the individual brand is a master brand. I noted "Weed Eater" as a name that was synonymous with string trimmers. I was astonished, then, to see a Weed Eater brand leaf blower. A Weed Eater is not a leaf blower, it's a . . . well, it's a weed eater, that's what! Using that name as a family brand is inappropriate for products other than those that pulverize the weeds around fence posts and such a strategy can only undermine the master brand position in the string trimmer category.

Line Extensions

Line extensions are a variation of turning an individual brand into something akin to a family brand. Advantages of the strategy are similar to those of family branding, namely quick recognition and acceptance. In the short term, that translates to lower costs than what would be necessary to launch a new brand. In the long run, however, you run the risk of destroying the uniqueness of the individual brand and with that, its distinctive position in the customer's mind.

When Anheuser-Busch decided to take on Miller Lite in the light beer category, they first tried the individual brand approach. The strategy was logical: Position a product directly against Miller Lite and their customers. The execution, in choice of a name, was a bit of a problem: "Anheuser-Busch Natural Light." It was all well and good to emphasize superior ingredients but not with a product whose name was eight syllables long. Ask a customer which product has top-of mind awareness in the low-cal, low-carb beer segment, and you're not going to have them give you a name eight syllables long when "Miller Lite" has three and "Lite" has just one. Further complicating the matter, imagine one of their high priority heavy users swaggering up to the bar around midnight at Butch's Back Room and trying to come out with an eight-syllable order to the barmaid. Anheuser-Busch tried to repair the damage by hiring language-wrecking Norm Crosby as spokesperson, urging customers to ask for a three-syllable "Natural," but the turkey wouldn't fly. So they line-extended but initially still failed to get the name right, starting with the four-syllable "Budweiser

Light" before finally figuring it all out and going with Bud Light, which has contended as they hoped it would.

The Coca-Cola Company faced a similar situation in the diet cola segment. Initially unwilling to line-extend their flagship brand, they attempted to compete with individual brand Tab against line extension Diet Pepsi. Finally, the decision was made to line-extend with the catchy name "Diet Coke," yielding much better results in the category.

A strong case can be made that line extension undermines the position of an individual brand, and marketing managers should approach line-extending with caution. Line extension should not be undertaken, or limited in scope, if it is apparent there will be long-term negative implications to such a strategy. In this regard, there are lessons to be learned from the American automobile industry.

There was a time when a Chevrolet meant an entry-level car, two-door, four-door, or wagon. Now, Chevrolet is a family brand of all sorts of cars and trucks plus, at the top end, the Corvette. However, each member of the family has its own identity. Trucks are most associated with the family brand as "Chevy trucks," the Corvette is the strongest individual brand, and the other cars are somewhere in the middle, having a distinct name but not an identity as strong as the Corvette. And except for the Corvette, which is a low-volume flagship and showpiece, the products are at the lower end for price and prestige. Previously, though, GM's philosophy had been to offer a wide range of product alternatives in every division. The idea was that if a prospect dropped into any GM dealership there would be a car to meet their needs, from big cars at the Chevy stores to compacts at Cadillac stores. In theory that sounded good but not in practice. Customers balked at high-end Chevys, figuring for that kind of money at least they should get a Buick. But the worst consequence was the impact of the Cimarron—a Cavalier with leather seats and a hood ornament—on traditional prospects at Cadillac dealerships, whose reaction was "*That's* a Cadillac? If that's a Cadillac, I'm going elsewhere!"

Line extension and family branding may be viable if the name has some meaning to the customer but a name cannot include all things for all people or it may end up meaning nothing to anybody. A unique new product absolutely commands its own name. For anything else, be careful to weigh long-term negatives against the short-term benefits.

Chapter 9

Strategic Considerations

To this point I've discussed the process of gathering information, identifying and describing target markets, and the basics about products and brands. Now the strategy can begin to take shape as managers determine which segments to address with what products.

In this chapter I'll address three major strategic considerations that will affect the specifies of the marketing plan: adopter categories and the Product Life Cycle, the new product development process, and strategic alternatives.

Adopter Categories and the Product Life Cycle

The product life cycle (PLC) is the graphic depiction of the sales and profit history of a product category (automobiles, aspirin, soft drinks), an individual brand (Oldsmobile, Bayer, Coca-Cola), or a specific product item (Cutlass two-door coupe, 81 mg caplets, 16-oz. returnable bottle). The concept is modeled after the biological life cycle of birth, growth, maturity, and demise. The PLC is a fundamental concept in the marketing profession, providing valuable insight for all four Ps (product/place/promotion/price). The most useful strategic implications derive from the PLC for the product category as a whole. Tactical decisions at the organization level address brands and product.

A PLC graph has two lines: sales and profits. Many marketing professionals think of the PLC solely as a sales history but it's essential to include category profits as well when you develop a marketing strategy. You may be inclined to enter a category whose sales are increasing at an increasing rate until you discover that category profits are near zero and dropping fast.

Also, it's important to note that, contrary to the biological life cycle, demise and death are not inevitable. There's no end in sight for categories such as information technology or professional medical services. Nor is death inevitable for individual brands as long as management continues to support the brand with updated product items and promotional activity. Two classic hundred-year-old success stories come to mind. Gillette introduced its original steel blade in 1903, a product item that had peaked and begun to decline by 1932, when they introduced the blue blade. All of a sudden, like an airplane that had stalled and restarted its engines, the sales for the brand accelerated. Gillette has continued to restart the brand engines over the years, most recently with two-blade razors, three-blade razors, and now four-blade razors. What can possibly be next? Whatever it is, Gillette is committed to maintaining upward momentum in its flagship brand and probably will succeed.

The sales history for the brand Coca-Cola is remarkably similar. Starting in 1899 and for over fifty years, the product was sold only in a six-ounce returnable bottle. The sales curve appeared to be peaking and heading for decline but then along came larger sizes, cans, and plastic bottles, and up went sales to higher and higher levels.

For the discussion that follows I will describe the PLC for a typical product category. Please note: specific categories, brands and product items may vary considerably in their sales/profit histories.

On Day One of a product category launch sales are by definition zero and profits are negative. This is the beginning of the introductory stage of the PLC. Sales increase at an increasing rate and, at the point where pre-intro fixed costs have been covered and the category moves into the black, the PLC enters the growth stage.

Sales increase throughout the growth stage, initially at an increasing rate and then at a decreasing rate. Profits peak near the end of the growth stage, and the point at which profits establish a definitive long-term downtrend marks the end of the growth stage and the beginning of maturity.

Sales continue to increase at a slow rate at the very beginning of the maturity stage and then reverse. Profits continue to steadily decline. At some point, usually with the introduction of a superior alternative, sales and profits reach a level sufficiently low that the category is considered to have entered the decline stage.

That's a quick overview of the four stages of the PLC. Now let's get down to details and possible exceptions in the profit component.

Introductory Stage
Every new product category starts its sales history at zero and profits negative as a reflection of R&D, costs of establishing production, and upfront expenses representing the price of admission into the game. Let's remember, now, that the beginning of the introductory stage is the moment when the category innovator opens the category as the sole player in it. There's a strong advantage to being first: it's the best chance for becoming the master brand, category leader in the customer's mind. But there's a flip side: you may encounter a learning curve that saps your profits while simultaneously educating and enlightening market followers who will soon be your competition. Do keep in mind that all those negative profits for the category on Day One are *your money*, and before making the plunge into those untested waters, be sure you have a high level of confidence in your gut-feel educated guess that you're going to be able to enjoy a healthy return on that initial investment.

Your opening salvo is likely to include a limited number of product items that can be expanded or line-extended over time. A personal selling blitz will be necessary to attain distribution of those primary product items among highest priority customers. Let's consider two contrasting situations.

For a consumer nondurable, the initial objective might be to reach a high level (90%+) of distribution in its primary channel, which could be retail grocery outlets. This will necessitate trade calls on buyers at all major chains, independents, wholesalers, and cooperatives, with a follow-up call at the outlet level to handle details of shelf space, displays, pricing, and point-of-sale. All this must be done in a very short time frame since the clock is ticking until the moment a competitive offering hits the streets. That accomplished, distribution can be expanded to outlets of secondary priority. From there product modifications may possibly improve the product or there may be enhancements in its manufacturing process, all a part of continuous improvement. New product items can be brought on line.

For a business-to-business (B2B) product or service, the personal selling blitz would likewise target top priority customers and prospects. Management would set a measurable objective of businesses to be called on and in what time frame. As in the case of consumer nondurables, later calls would address secondary priorities and, over time, more product items.

Introductory pricing will be determined according to the long-term objectives of the organization. I'll discuss pricing—the fourth "P"—in the final chapter. At this point, let's just say that the firm is making an investment of money and manpower in the hope and expectation of maximizing its long-term profitability.

Since the initiator of a product category is offering something new, the objective of early advertising will be to inform prospects about the category and its benefits. As long as the initiator is unchallenged by a competitive offering their product *is* the category, so the objective of the informative advertising is to educate the prospect, create primary demand—demand for the category per se—and create a category leadership position in the prospect's mind.

Those very first people to try a new product, the adopter category known as innovators, are a different breed of cat. Knowing what these people are like, and effectively communicating with them, is helpful for a two-dollar convenience product and absolutely essential for high-involvement decisions or B2B products.

Innovators constitute about two or three percent of customers but it's these people who get the missile off the launch pad, so to speak. Innovators think for themselves, unrestrained by habitual norms of their colleagues or society. They don't rely on the input of others to try something new because, of course, they try it before anyone else does.

Innovators tend to be young, more cosmopolitan, better educated, and earn higher incomes than their peers. Especially for a high-involvement purchase, they will tend to hear about the category from independent business and scientific sources. Their opinion leaders include experts who can provide information and insight about this new category. An example of an innovator is that guy you know in the city who was using the Internet before anybody else even knew what the Internet was. Marketers initiating a category must think about innovators when developing their promotional plans. Innovators are not to be reached only through traditional media. Plan for publicity and the dissemination of information through independent professional sources.

Depending on the nature of the product and the organization's strategic objectives there may be high levels of promotional activity during the introductory stage to gain consumer trial. However, for a breakthrough product with, as yet, no competitive alternatives, such promotions may be dealbacks from artificially high prices. Open with a retail price of $4.99, have a "special promotion" of a dollar off, and offer the product at retail for $3.99, which is the high entry-level price you wanted in the first place. These promotional considerations will also be addressed in detail in Chapter 13: Pricing.

As you move through the introductory stage sales are increasing at a rapid rate and, since you're all alone in the category with a 100% share, you may be inclined to categorize your product as a Star: high share in a high growth market. But not so fast. Because you're starting from a zero base, of course your early week-to-week sales increases look good on a percentage basis. The key question, though, is: are sales increasing satisfactorily in *absolute* terms, in line with or ahead of forecast? If not, you do not have a high-share product in a low-growth market— a Cash Cow—you have a new product failure—a turkey—which should be taken out back behind the shed and dispatched forthwith.

On the other hand, if absolute sales are strong you can expect that competitors will soon be in the fray, all of whom will enter as Question Marks starting at a zero share in a high-growth segment. The ability of competitors to enter the market, and in what time frame, will be a significant consideration of your marketing plan, especially for pricing.

About halfway through the introductory stage of the PLC the next adopter group begins to emerge: the early adopters, the next 12–15% to adopt the product. These folks are considerably more oriented to group and social norms than the independently-minded innovators and, of importance to marketers, tend to hold leadership positions in the community, command the respect of others, and are the opinion leaders who will most influence the adopter groups that follow.

A product category enters the growth stage of the PLC when about a third of those who will adopt the product have done so. As noted, in general this is about the point where the category moves into net profitability. By this time, it is very likely that competitors have entered the market, so a net break-even profitability for the category translates into some net profits for the initiator balanced by some net losses for the followers. This point—the one-third mark of product diffusion—is an appropriate time to gauge profit prospects for the category over the long term. If the category is not yet yielding profits and the break-even point is still far off on the horizon, red lights should go on. It's getting late early. Managers facing such a situation must start asking tough questions about whether the category will *ever* get in the black and whether further investments amount to shoveling sand into a sinkhole. As a general rule, intensity of promotion diminishes as a product enters the growth stage. Sales promotion in the introductory stage enticed trail. Now, entering the growth stage, your hope and expectation is to enjoy a period of profitable sales before the market matures, competition becomes entrenched, and the promotion battle for market share gets underway. If, however, promotion from competitors has already begun to intensify at the onset of the growth stage and profits remain somewhere in the indeterminate future, consider the possibility that the category may never achieve significant long-term profitability.

Halfway through the growth stage of the PLC the product has been adopted by the next group, the early majority. Innovators and early adopters combined account for about the first one-sixth of those who will ultimately adopt the product. The early majority alone accounts for twice that, another one-third of eventual adopters, defining the point at which half of those who will adopt the product have done so.

The early majority can be profiled as solid middle-class consumers, open to new ideas but not inclined to be one of the first in the water. They will take their time to gather information and comparison shop. By the time the early majority has adopted it, the product has diffused to the point where it's become a familiar part of the national scene.

The next large group of adopters, the late majority, is also about one third of those who will ultimately adopt the product. By the time they've all adopted about five-sixths of those who will ever join the category have done so. During this period, as the total product diffusion moves from the 50% level to the 83% level, dramatic changes will take place in the marketing environment as the category moves out of the growth stage of the PLC and into the maturity stage.

Persons of the late majority are often older with below average education and income. They tend to be conservative, traditional, and disinclined to consider new products, ideas, or ways of doing things. For high-tech new products, however, many persons in the late majority will be of above average education and income but unfamiliar and uncomfortable with technology. Those in the latter stages of the late majority can be motivated by social and peer pressures to get on board, conformity being important to traditional, conservative consumers. Since they are skeptical of new products these people will shop carefully, compare alternatives, and will be inclined to enter a category once a certain price point is reached. In the maturity stage of the PLC competition is intense and promotional pressures increase. By this point the only way to increase sales is by taking market share away from competition, so prices are pressured downward, attracting the price-sensitive late majority. Profits fall throughout the maturity stage.

In contrast to overall trends, niche entries at the high end of a product class tend to emerge in the maturity stage, especially in consumer nondurables. Starbucks took that approach in coffee, the micro breweries in beer, and, on the other end of the scale, the late great Concorde in air travel. Fads may enhance that opportunity. The low-carb line extensions in the ice cream market were excluded from sales promotions in many areas during their introductory summer in hopes that consumers caught up in the craze would pay the everyday price.

Finally, as a product enters the latter part of the maturity stage, the final one-sixth of adopters—laggards—come into the category. Laggards tend to be older persons who feel alienated by a rapidly-changing society, suspicious of anything new. Don't depend on them ever becoming profitable heavy users.

Of course no matter what happens some people, the nonadopters, never do join the category. Yes, some people do still have rabbit ears on their TV set and cut their two-acre lawn with a non-motorized lawn mower.

As a category enters dotage, the decline stage of the PLC, only a core group of loyal users remain. Marginal players drop out of the market, leaving one, or at most two, serious organizations still active in the segment. Advertising and sales promotion are radically reduced or eliminated entirely as marketers seek to milk the cow of every last drop in the tank. At some point—earlier I noted the example of typewriter repair—the segment is no longer worth anyone's while. Forward-looking firms have moved on to new opportunities in new markets. Firms lacking vision and foresight, muddling along in a production orientation, fall by the wayside and perish.

The product life cycle and adopter categories are two of the most important concepts in marketing. I'll revisit them in the chapters on advertising and pricing.

The New Product Development Process

By now it should be apparent that there are limited opportunities with existing products and that firms must regularly update the product mix. In some cases new product strategy may be as simple as a me-too match of a competitive offering. Current product lines may be improved and expanded. Hopefully, a firm's new product strategy will lead to the development of breakthrough products with a competitive advantage not easily copied in the short term, creating a leadership position in the customer's mind. There are, however, very few monumental new-to-the-world products, known among academics as "discontinuous innovations," product categories such as the telephone, television, and the Internet. Most new products will be improvements of existing items or additions of new items to extend the PLC of an existing brand. But *something* must be new to use the term "new." The all-new 1979 Cutlass had redesigned taillights, after all.

Stage 1: Idea Generation

A proactive organization maintains a continuous search for new product ideas consistent with overall strategic objectives and target market needs. Thus input is encouraged from all employees, and particularly the sales force, as well as customers and channel partners. Although idea generation should not be restricted to the company headquarters ivory tower, formal new product brainstorming sessions probably will take place at a centralized location. There's one fundamental rule in these brainstorming sessions: no one is too fast on the trigger, ready to shoot down an idea.

If a new product is truly new it may seem unusual or strange. People may be quick to say it's stupid or impractical. Competition may have briefly considered an idea and rejected it as unfeasible. Fine, no problem. It still can be considered. It still rates a page on the flip chart, plastered with all the others around and around the room. I've been in several of these organized brainstorming sessions and am always amazed at how, an hour later, someone will come back to a page on the wall, virtually ridiculed earlier, and suddenly take a point, extend it a step, and a viable concept was born. When you brainstorm anything and everything can be considered.

Stage 2: Idea Screening

Brainstorming is designed to get the creative juices flowing but idea screening quickly filters those ideas down to reality. Some ideas, though they have merit, are inconsistent with the organization's objectives and capabilities. It is especially important to consider the implications of diversifying into unknown territory or embarking into new channels of distribution. A company that manufactures batteries may not have the capability of producing alternators. A newspaper publisher may have the capability of publishing a magazine but lack the expertise and resources to make the venture succeed.

At this stage, it might be helpful to conduct concept tests for either a new product or an advertising campaign. If it could be produced at a reasonable cost a laboratory sample of the proposed product could be presented to potential customers, perhaps in a focus group, to get an idea of what they think about it and whether they would have an interest in it. Just keep in mind the limitations of focus groups and the low reliability of "intention to buy" questions. Ad campaigns can be screened through the use of storyboards, a commercial formatted as a comic strip, to gauge reaction to a proposed concept and message, especially one that is unique or controversial. Storyboards can be created by an artist in a day, at negligible cost. Should target market reaction turn out to be negative you just saved the very significant investment of producing a commercial and buying wasted media.

Stage 3: Business Analysis

If everything's still looking good now's the time to run some numbers, forecasting sales, estimating profitability, and doing a break-even analysis. There are numerous sophisticated analytical tools for forecasting sales, none a whole lot better than your best gut-felt educated guess. Just don't do a sales forecast in isolation. Think through the proportion of new product sales that will be incremental sales compared to sales that cannibalize existing items. Yes, that's a guesstimate but your personal expertise is superior to any analytical tool. Ask yourself: Will this product really generate new business or merely replace the old? And if all it does is replace the old, is that bad? One more consideration: Don't forget to make a best guess about the competitive response to your new entry. You can have a high level of confidence that the competition will not just take a wait-and-see approach to your activities.

The first three stages of the new product development process are reasonably inexpensive but beyond this point costs increase exponentially. And the fact is that from this point forward, at least 80%—and likely closer to 90%—of new product ideas will have failed within a year of full-scale commercialization. This is the time to take a step back and ask yourself whether the new product concept is really superior to 80% or 90% of the ideas you've seen. If it's not, the time to kill it is now. Certainly, if the idea does not clearly stand among the top 50%, it is unlikely to offer viability.

Stage 4: Development

The decision to move into development represents a serious commitment of resources. Barring unexpected events this is tantamount to a "Go" for moving into test marketing. Engineering and R&D people now proceed to produce a prototype product as their marketing colleagues finalize details concerning the product name, packaging, pricing, and introductory promotions. The advertising staff goes to work creating TV, radio, outdoor, print, and point-of-sale materials.

Some products, particularly consumer nondurables and industrial supplies, may undergo in-home and on-the-job sampling at this stage. Inputs from users help marketers make product refinements that more effectively address target market needs. Major product problems would not be expected at this stage but if they occur, better now than in test marketing. Easily tested would be alternative product formulations and packaging.

Years ago I was working with a consumer products company that had developed a carbonated sweet tea. Consumer reaction at the development stage was so overwhelmingly negative that product modifications were out of the question and the product was killed. However, such a strongly negative result should never have happened in the development phase. This turkey should have been shot down in idea screening, saving the squandering of considerable time and resources.

Stage 5: Test Marketing

With development completed you have a product that could conceivably be launched nationwide tomorrow. Anxious to get on with it some marketers, 100% confident of success, propose skipping test marketing entirely or substituting with a laboratory test. That's a mistake. Data from a laboratory test cannot yield a valid representation of a total market experience. The validity of laboratory tests is limited to one or at most a very few variables in a controlled experiment. Furthermore, if handled properly test marketing can yield extremely valuable data on advertising, pricing, and promotion. The time and resources for test marketing are a good investment.

Test marketing involves a full-scale product launch into limited areas, generally three or four cities, to monitor sales performance and customer reactions in an actual market situation. Mainstream products tend to be test marketed in heartland cities such as Columbus or Spokane, whereas products targeted at specific groups would conduct tests in markets where target market population is most dense. For example, a product targeted at Hispanics might restrict test marketing to cities in the south and southwest.

To optimize the value of test marketing, employ different levels of marketing variables in the respective markets. For instance, have high, medium, and low levels for pricing, sales promotion, and advertising. Then structure the test markets with different mixes of those variables to determine the optimum combination. An analysis of variance might conclude, as an example, that the combination of high price/medium promotion/high advertising would best achieve organization objectives. You cannot generate such valuable data with a simulated laboratory test.

Naturally, the bottom line number for test marketing is sales and its comparison with your gut-feel educated guess forecast. Here's another moment when a brutal assessment of reality is called for. Sure, you've invested a lot of time and money to get this far but unless sales meet or exceed forecast not much will be gained by living in denial and hoping that things will be different in a national rollout. They won't. Detach yourself from all your emotions and pull the plug.

I remember one test marketing where management's refusal to confront reality cost them in the low eight figures. I was analyzing sales results from their four test market cities and projected the product could expect a national sales level of 6.5 million cases a year if it achieved 100% distribution. Management came back to me and insisted I revise the estimate, saying that the decision had already been made to go national no matter what the results were in the test markets, and they needed a number of at least 25 million cases. I was astonished, spent a few moments asking myself why they were paying me to do this, and complied. The test market data had indicated that the average user would consume one unit of product per month. I calculated the range, at a 99% probability, was between 0.25 and four units per month, took the number at the high end of the range, and quadrupled the usage rate to give them a high-end sales projection of 26 million cases. They did not wish me to include the low-end number, 1.6 million cases, which was equally likely. The product was launched into national distribution and soon died a natural death. Until the very end, the brand manager truly believed a miracle would occur and the product would catch on. Don't let this happen to you or your organization. If test marketing doesn't give you an unequivocal yes, detach with love and call an end to the game. It's a "no."

Stage 6: Rollout
This, of course, is what you're hoping for. It's a "yes." Go for it.

Why New Products Fail

Since the vast majority of new products fail at some stage in the new product development process or shortly after rollout, it's important to note the major reasons for failure. It seems so simple, but the most important reason why new products fail is because the target market neither wants nor needs them. Closely related to that, the products have no differential advantages over competitive alternatives. Almost always product failures were unable to find a position in the customer's mind, an objective unattainable without a definitive product benefit or unique and distinctive extrinsics.

Throughout this book I've stressed the need for proper execution and implementation. Despite this need many otherwise good products fail for all the wrong reasons. Recently a major food products company launched a new product with a blitz of TV advertising and Sunday supplement coupons. The only problem was that when would-be customers went to the stores the product wasn't on the shelves. The company's meager introductory offer had been rejected by all the major chains, none of whom had authorized the product. It is unthinkable that a major company would not have known the trade's standards for accepting a new product into distribution, and validated their assumptions and expectations in test markets.

Another classic failure was a company's aggressive program to expand the market for tapioca pudding, with their product taking the leadership position. Highly optimistic sales projections were confirmed in test markets and the product got the green light for national rollout. Only then did the company discover that its ingredients requirements exceeded the world's total production of tapioca and that they were unable to get sufficient product on the shelves.

High-tech products often fail due to flaws that lie undiscovered until some time after launch. Autos from the Corvair to high-profile SUVs have experienced sudden sales problems on the raising of safety concerns. A complaint from the Consumer Product Safety Commission can throw a monkey wrench into the best-laid plans.

And finally, sometimes a new product idea is just too early or just too late. A few years ago Sears decided to discontinue its catalogue, deeming the direct channel nonviable. Just a few years later they discovered that the direct channel was growing by leaps and bounds, but through the Internet. Had events evolved differently they would have been able to make a smooth transition from the traditional catalogue to an Internet-based system. Timing of the Internet revolution was not favorable for Sears but they've adapted. That's a lot better situation than being too late, when an organization takes a wait-and-see attitude and, when they finally do decide to act, the market's already passed them by and someone else has taken the leadership position and all the profits.

Strategic Alternatives

As you see, a great deal of thought goes in to segmenting markets and developing products to address customer needs. Now, with a product portfolio in place, marketers can finalize tactics designed to achieve strategic objectives.

Category and Brand Development Indices
The Boston Consulting Group (BCG) matrix was helpful in profiling products in relation to the total marketplace. Now let's look at another matrix that helps you understand market differences and their strategic implications at the local level. This matrix can be developed by calculating a market's category development index (CDI) and brand development index (BDI), easily derived from syndicated data such as that available through the A.C. Nielsen Company.

The CDI calculates the relative importance of a total product category as a percentage of total dollars spent in the measured outlet class. By definition the national CDI is 100. Let's look at an example using Nielsen data for the outlet class of food stores. For every $100 in food store sales Product Class X accounts for 50¢, so product class sales of 50¢ per $100 would define a CDI of 100. In local market A Product Class X only accounts for 40¢ of every $100 spent, so the CDI is 40¢ ÷ 50¢, or 80. A CDI of 80 or less would be considered a "Low CDI" market, meaning the category is less well developed than the national average. By contrast, in local market B Product Class X accounts for 65¢ of every $100 spent, so its CDI is 65¢ ÷ 50¢, or 130. A CDI of 120 or more is considered a "High CDI" market, meaning the category is better developed than the national average. So, out of, say, fifty markets, fifteen or so are low CDI, fifteen or so are high CDI, and the remaining twenty somewhere in the middle. By the way, there's nothing inflexible about the choice of 80 or less for low CDI and 120 or more for high CDI. If you wish use 90 and 110, or 70 and 130, or whatever.

BDI is a similar calculation, though for the brand instead of the category. Using the same data, let's say that Brand K, your entry in Product Class X, accounts for 20¢ of every $100 in food store sales nationally. Thus, brand sales of 20¢ per $100 would define a BDI of 100. By the way, you may have noticed that share of market can be directly calculated from these data. If Product Class X accounts for 50¢ of $100 in total outlet sales and Brand K, an entry in Product Class X, accounts for 20¢ of $100, the share of market for Brand K is 20¢ ÷ 50¢, or 40%.

In local market A, let's say Brand K accounts for 16¢ of every $100 spent. Its BDI is 16¢ ÷ 20¢, or 80, making it a "Low BDI" market. However, it's important to note that market A is also a low CDI market and that the share of market for Brand K is 16¢ ÷ 40¢, or 40%, exactly its national share.

By contrast, in local market B Brand K accounts for 24¢ of every $100 spent, so its BDI is 24¢ ÷ 20¢, or 120, classifying it as a "High BDI" market. However, since the CDI for local market B—130—is even higher than the BDI, share of market for Brand K is lower than its national average: 24¢ ÷ 65¢, or 37%.

Here's how marketing managers can apply CDI and BDI for local market strategies. First, naturally, they should identify reasons why any local market has a share lower than its national average. In other words, why is the BDI less than the CDI? It's easy to miss that looking at sales alone. Initially, managers may be pleased that a brand's per capita sales in a market are 40% more than the national average, a BDI of 140. However, if the CDI is 160, their brand is falling behind. Let's consider two possible scenarios.

Scenario 1: CDI is very high (160) due to strong marketing of private label brands by the major chains. Your leading competitor has a BDI of only 130, less than your BDI of 140. The competitive situation is reasonably favorable, and suggests an opportunity to persuade the trade to consider more promotional activity and strong in-outlet presence for your products compared to private labels.

Scenario 2: The CDI is very high (160) because your leading competitor has a BDI of 200 and is running away with the market. The competitive situation is very unfavorable and this is a local market in need of attention. Why is this happening, and what can you do to wrench the leadership position away from them?

Addressing situations one local market at a time ultimately adds up to performance at a national level. It's just one more example of building a strategy from the bottom up.

Viewing markets in a high/low CDI/BDI matrix is also helpful in profiling markets and suggesting local strategies. Let's look at the four combinations.

HIGH CDI/HIGH BDI: GOLD MINES. You have strong sales in a market where the category is well developed. This translates to trade receptivity for the category and your brand and suggests a good "bang for the buck" for promotions, new products, and intensified marketing activities. Take a leadership role in the category and its growth with a goal of at least equaling the BDI of your major competitor and then steadily increasing the distance between you and them.

HIGH CDI/LOW BDI: TARGETS OF OPPORTUNITY. These markets are crises demanding immediate attention. How can it be that the category is well developed and your sales are underdeveloped? For some reason customers have embraced the category but rejected you. Determine whether it's private labels or the competition that's taken the leadership role and why it is you're not in the game.

LOW CDI/HIGH BDI: COMMANDOS. Just the opposite of High CDI/ Low BDI. You own the category and face minimal competitive threats. Take care of those loyal customers and play solid defense. Crush any competitive intrusions without mercy.

LOW CDI/LOW BDI: BASKET CASES. As a first check, be sure that your BDI is at least as high as the CDI, giving you a market share equal to or higher than your national average. Beyond that, particularly for very low CDIs of 60 or less, question the return on investment beyond a maintenance level unless you have reason to believe you can develop the market. More than likely your limited funds will be better spent in high CDI markets.

Modifications of the Product Mix

I've described the need to extend a product's life cycle rather than rely on new products. Toward that end professional marketers embrace the concept of continuous improvement, the ongoing effort to make products better and to produce them more efficiently. Such modifications make sense. However, modifying a product by repositioning it may not be a viable alternative to a new product and may be unsuccessful in trying to save a recalcitrant problem child or dawg.

Repositioning is most likely to work by making a product more inclusive, retaining satisfied customers who might otherwise move out of the market. Examples would include Johnson's Baby Shampoo in its appeal to young women interested in the benefits of a mild and gentle product, or Kellogg's Frosted Flakes, telling adults they'll love the cereal as much today as they did when they were kids. Radically repositioning a brand is far more difficult, though not impossible.

I was working with a consumer products company that was replacing a brand with a new product. Rather than delete the old product they tried to keep it alive with a new ad campaign designed to reposition the brand to women 35–49 instead of its former prime segment, men 25–39. The effort burned a lot of resources and failed. An ad campaign alone was not enough to shift the position of the same product in the customer's mind.

General Motors tried to reposition Oldsmobile as something more than your grandfather's car but was unsuccessful in doing so and the brand was dropped. That's in contrast to a similar strategy for Cadillac, accompanied by several lines of vehicles that have won over target markets of young affluent buyers. The cost of saving the Cadillac brand has been considerable but a good investment.

Continuous improvement is a given. Beyond that marketers must carefully weigh alternatives of line extensions, new products, and the repositioning of old products. There's no one right answer and no magic formula but that's why they pay you the big bucks.

Strategies for Targeting Markets

With the product portfolio ready to go, and target market segments identified, there's just one more process of filtering to do: Decide if there are segments you're *not* going to go for after all. This is particularly important for a single product that is marketed to different markets solely on the basis of extrinsics. Examples of this are Harley-Davidson marketing its motorcycles to seven separate segments and Porsche marketing its sports cars to five. Also, it is possible that certain segments will be similar with comparable product needs and can combined and treated as one segment. Finally, managers may decide that a certain product and segment no longer have sufficient potential and should be dropped. Those decisions made, management elects to approach the marketplace with one of three strategies.

Undifferentiated Target Market Strategy
An undifferentiated strategy is a "One for all and all for one" approach, targeting all segments with the same product and the same marketing mix. Though such a strategy provides the organization savings in its production and marketing costs, it is an example of a production orientation, leaving a firm vulnerable to a competitor who differentiates. As noted earlier, the undifferentiated market strategy served Henry Ford well through the early days of the PLC for the automobile and for Coca-Cola through the first half of the 20th century. But today trying to be everything to everyone means you're nothing to anyone in consumer marketing.

Concentrated Target Market Strategy
In a concentrated market strategy a firm elects to address only one target market, creating a marketing mix designed to serve that market's special needs. The philosophy of this approach is to go where the business is, directing all the firm's resources on the one target of opportunity. It may also mean seeking an unoccupied position in a small portion of a large market: NyQuil wants to be the cold medication you take at night. Enterprise wants to be the rental car company for non-business customers whose car is in for repairs.

Concentrated targeting to a small market segment is known as niche marketing, often an opportunity for small organizations that want to specialize in segments small enough that larger competitors will leave them alone. No one competes with Rolls-Royce or Rolex at the extreme high end of their categories and those firms have such a strong hold of the prestige position in the customer's mind that it's not worth the effort and investment to attempt to assault the mountain.

Niche marketing is the opposite of the majority fallacy, the strategy of going after the largest segment of the market just like everyone else. Lava is everything other soaps *aren't* and it owns its segment uncontested. Why not consider brainstorming a similar niche position for your product category, whatever it is? If your product category is "only for women," the position for a product directed at men is yours for the taking. "Only African-Americans would use that" should cause a light to go on, telling you that 85% of the market is unserved. Now, certainly, some products are only for specific demographic segments or target markets. An uncontested segment may offer limited sales potential. You might determine that a particular niche could never exceed one-half of one percent in total market share. Fine! Calculate what one-half of one percent of a category translates to in annual sales. It might be worth your while to address such a niche segment, take the leadership position, and hold the top of the mountain in terrain small enough to defend.

Multisegment Target Market Strategy
With a multisegment strategy the firm addresses more than one target market using a separate marketing mix for each. It is tantamount to multiple concentrated strategies. Technically my earlier examples of seven segments for Harley-Davidson and five for Porsche are multisegment strategies, although the first "P" of the marketing mix—Product—is the same for all segments. Multisegment marketing is the game the big companies play, though if you segment the same product solely through extrinsics with different messages in different media the strategy can be affordable for smaller firms.

The multisegment strategy targets one segment with Stouffer's Gourmet Entrees and another with Lean Cuisine, one segment with Budweiser and another with Michelob Ultra, one segment with button-fly blue jeans and another with Dockers. Line extensions usually represent an attempt to address an specific market segment with a variation of product and message, and succeeds to the extent that the line extension achieves incremental sales or takes business away from competitors. Generally, however, line extensions heavily cannibalize the mother brand. Sales for Liquid Tide came predominantly from Tide, not other liquids. Sales for Diet Coke came mostly from Coca-Cola, not other diet colas.

New products marketed as individual brands will have less cannibalization than line extensions, even in examples with few product differences. Slim Fast and Ensure are similar products, the former positioned as a diet aid and the latter as a dietary supplement. I'm waiting for a new version to be marketed under the name Beefcake, for guys to drink during and after workouts. Similar product but its own name and unique positioning to its target market.

Summing Up

Developing and executing a marketing strategy is a whole lot more than throwing something over the fence and hoping for the best. Strategy necessitates learning everything about the product class, the nature of the market, and an understanding of how customer needs can be satisfied. The right new products must be developed in the right way and tested in a manner that prepares them for rollout with the marketing mix best able to achieve sales and profit objectives. Different situations must be identified in the field and exploited at the local level, adding up to success in the aggregate.

One last point: The strategic process is dynamic, not static. Managers do not merely develop products and programs, send them out to the marketplace, and wait for the results. The strategy evolves day by day. Every day, tactics are modified. Target market assessment, portfolio modifications, and new product development are all part of a continuous loop. Change is a constant that guarantees tomorrow will not look like today. Persons and organizations that discover those changes and the opportunities they present can seize the moment, become first in the customer's mind, and take the leadership position.

CHAPTER 10

Channels and Retailing

It's time for "P" number two: Place, including channels and distribution. Included under this umbrella are all the people, places, and activities between you and the ultimate consumer. Channels and retailing are critical elements in the execution of your marketing plan. Never develop product strategies in isolation. Consider the other three Ps and how they complement the product: promotion, pricing, and especially place/distribution.

In making distribution decisions, managers may eliminate intermediaries, but cannot eliminate the functions they perform. The next time someone tells you, "We've eliminated the middleman," be sure to correct them by saying, "No, you have elected to perform those activities the middlemen would have conducted on your behalf." The old Soviet Union considered middlemen to be parasites, "speculators" who acted in opposition to the best interests of the proletariat and thus earned a trip to the gulag. As a result, in the village that had a factory making candlesticks, citizens stood on street corners trying to sell candlesticks while in the next village, with a factory that made cutlery, citizens had booths selling steak knives. Since wholesalers and retailers were considered profiteers and enemies of the people, citizens enjoyed an hour in line at the bread store, another hour in line at the dairy store, and so forth until the entire day was wasted shopping for the evening meal.

Early in the book I described the concept of specialization and differential advantage noting that individuals and organizations should concentrate on what they do best, then outsource to specialists those functions outside their area of expertise. The alternative perspective was to be an outsourcer, performing a special function for a variety of clients. The same points of competitive advantage are valid for distribution decisions. It is more efficient to outsource those functions to specialists.

Direct channels, including Internet-based e-commerce, are inherently inefficient. They necessitate contact with each and every individual, whereas a relationship with a retail store enables a marketer to serve dozens, hundreds, or even thousands of ultimate consumers through one contact. Additionally, it is far less costly to deliver a truckload of merchandise to a wholesaler or a retail outlet than it is to ship individual packages to individual customers. That does not mean there is anything wrong with direct channels, only that advantages in other elements of the marketing mix must more than offset inefficiencies in distribution.

Distribution Functions and Channel Structure

Depending on the product you market certain distribution functions must be performed to bring the product from its point of production to the point of encounter with the ultimate consumer. For all products you must determine the channel structure, specifying which distribution functions you will mange internally and which functions will be outsourced to specialists. Let's first discuss physical distribution functions.

Accumulating

Accumulating, also known as accumulating bulk, is a function designed to address discrepancies of quantity resulting from producers whose quantities are of insufficient size for the next step in the production chain. This function is often associated with agricultural products. An accumulator might buy the crop of several small growers of oranges and then sell them by the truckload to the processor, who will not buy in less-than-truckload quantities.

Bulk-Breaking

Bulk-breaking is the opposite of accumulating: a wholesaler buys a truckload of oranges, now in ten-pound bags, and sells them by the pallet or split pallet to retailers. Bulk-breaking would be equally appropriate for nonagricultural products.

Assorting

Assorting is the process of combining products from many different sources to be conveniently available at one location. This is what wholesalers and retailers do and, contrary to the attitudes of the old Soviet Union, why we're happy to let the supermarket enjoy a profit margin so we don't have to spend all day standing in lines.

Drop Shippers

Drop shippers are wholesalers who take ownership but not possession of the goods they sell, acting more like an agent. They deal predominantly in commodities such as coal and non-perishable agricultural products. Here's what they do: Let's say there's a coal producer in West Virginia that mines a hundred-car load of coal. This producer doesn't yet have a buyer but rather than just letting the coal sit there, it starts the train heading west. About the time the train nears Columbus a drop shipper gets an order for twenty cars of coal from a buyer in Cleveland. The drop shipper purchases twenty cars in transit and at Columbus those cars are diverted to Cleveland while the remaining eighty continue west. As the train nears Indianapolis another drop shipper grabs thirty cars for a customer in Evansville, and so forth until the entire train is sold out. The drop shipper has performed a valuable service for the coal producer, permitting them to get inventory on the road and relieving them of having to deal with individual customers.

Rack Jobbers

Rack jobbers are wholesalers who, in effect, rent space in retail outlets and then manage and merchandise that space. They have become more important as retailers market non-traditional products they do not wish to handle directly. Rack jobbers originally managed those household gadgets found on pegs in the supermarket aisles. Now, they handle entire sections such as newspapers, magazines, and greeting cards. Consider greeting cards: The day after Thanksgiving, it's time to take out the Thanksgiving cards and put out the Christmas cards. The retail store doesn't want to mess with the task, and, of special concern, they have no space or facilities for storing all the unsold Thanksgiving cards until pulling them out again next year after Halloween.

Thus, for a rental fee and a share of the profit margin, the store hands the greeting card section over to the rack jobber.

Both drop shippers and rack jobbers are specialty outsourcers employing the benefit of competitive advantage, a superior alternative to either producers or retailers conducting those functions themselves. Marketers must make a similar assessment of differential advantage in deciding whether to use other channel specialists between themselves and the ultimate consumer.

Alternative Channel Arrangements

Generally, marketers make the decisions concerning channels and intermediaries. However, in some situations those decisions are imposed upon them because of the nature of the product or legal constraints. For example, by law alcoholic beverage companies cannot sell directly to stores but must market through independent wholesale distributors. Ultimate consumers must purchase their products at retail stores served by the distributors. Soft drink bottling companies are both protected and restricted by geographic territories granted by their parent companies. Bottlers may not sell outside their territories and retail stores must purchase from the bottling company in their location.

In a nutshell, either you perform all the distribution functions yourself—a direct channel such as catalogues by mail, "800" numbers on radio or TV, or an e-commerce business model—or you utilize intermediaries or specialists to handle some or all of the functions. There are four alternative channel arrangements.

Direct Channel

As noted, in a direct channel there are no intermediaries between the producer and consumer. Traditionally, little attention is paid to direct marketing in textbooks but today, especially due to the rapid growth of Internet-based selling, it cannot be overlooked. I'll discuss the direct channel in detail later in this chapter.

Retailer Channel

In a retailer channel, the marketer uses the services of a single intermediary, an organization with retail outlets that sell to the ultimate consumer. There are three different modes of retailer channels.

The first mode of retailer channel is marketer-owned retail stores, the tactic of vertical integration, a common example being factory outlet stores. Many tire companies own retail stores that feature their products exclusively plus offer related products and ancillary services.

The second mode of retailer channel is direct store delivery (DSD), a tactic of necessity for perishables such as bread and milk and a legal requirement for alcoholic beverage companies. DSD is the mode of choice for snack food and major soft drink companies. Although DSD is more expensive than shipping to the retailer's warehouse, sales rep presence at outlet level enhances merchandising and product presentation at the point of encounter and builds personal relationships with store managers. DSD marketers sell in products and promotions at outlet level to single-store independent retailers. For large chains, however, activities must first be authorized at headquarters or regional level. Individual store managers, then, have some authority concerning actions at outlet level, such as allocating space for special displays, but are generally not authorized to accept anything not pre-approved at a corporate level.

The third mode of retailer channel, the one the big marketers employ, also features headquarters or regional calls for authorization, but product is shipped through the retailer's warehouse rather than being delivered direct to the individual store. As a consequence, most stocking and product rotation, as well as cleaning of shelves and other housekeeping, must be done by store personnel. Naturally, store employees cannot be expected to manage a product section with standards as high as those for DSD salespeople and merchandisers. Therefore, a representative of the marketer may make a call at outlet level, once a month or so, to clean up the section, rotate stock and place new point-of-sale material.

Wholesaler Channel

There are two intermediaries in a wholesaler channel. The marketing company, instead of delivering product directly to a retailer's outlets or warehouse, goes through a wholesaler who is the retailer's source of supply. Big marketers who work predominantly through retailer channels will also utilize wholesaler channels to serve retail organizations too small to justify personalized calls.

Agent Channel
A marketing firm will utilize an agent channel, usually through a broker, when they elect to use contractors in lieu of their own employees to conduct selling functions. In turn, those agents represent the company's products through either a retailer or wholesaler channel. As a rule, organizations employing an agent channel are too small to be able to afford an independent sales force. However, in recent years numerous large marketers have eliminated their sales forces in favor of brokers. In the short run, such a decision looks good on a company's bottom line, helping management reach annual financial goals and reap the attendant rewards. However, there is no way a broker can represent the marketing firm in a chain call as well as an independent sales rep would, and the broker is not as motivated to negotiate satisfactory performance, terms, and conditions for promotional programs. Furthermore, brokers will not provide anywhere near the same level of attention at outlet level. As a result electing an agent channel over an independent sales force is likely to be detrimental in the longer term. Managers making such a decision are hopeful of being rewarded and gone before the chickens come home to roost.

In the B2B segment firms too small to afford an independent sales force will use contractors known as manufacturers' reps, selling related but noncompeting products to business customers. In the beverage industry, for example, one rep will call on a producer offering display equipment, cardboard cartons, and bottle caps, all of them needed by the customer but none of sufficient volume to be sold through individual company salespeople.

I'm often approached by entrepreneurs and small businesspeople interested in knowing how to go about attaining distribution for a product they wish to market. These persons and firms are too small to afford an independent sales force and would not be granted an appointment by a chain buyer, so an agent channel is the only option open to them. My advice is to identify the types of outlets they want to target and go into those places and talk to the retail manager. The objective of this very brief meeting is to learn who are the brokers and agents most suitable for doing the job and doing it right. Just a few meetings with retail outlet managers should generate a short list of those brokers and agents who would do the best job representing the product. Then, when contacting those agents and brokers, they can introduce themselves with a referral from a store manager to establish credibility and legitimacy. As in any agent relationship they must be sure to have an unambiguous written understanding of what this person will do on their behalf and how he or she will be compensated.

The same approach can be adopted to B2B products. Go to a typical target customer, likely someone who is a prospect for your product. Whether you sell them or not, ask about manufacturer's reps calling on them who would be good people to represent your product. Then, again with a referral, talk to those reps, learn something about their company, and determine whether there might be an opportunity for their organization to represent you in the B2B marketplace.

Channel Power

In channel relationships, as in life generally, everyone is out to get what's in their own best interest and the more power you have or are perceived as having, the more favorable the outcome will be. Thus, Wal-Mart as a retailer and Procter & Gamble as a producer are better able to specify terms and conditions than are the smaller players. Nevertheless, if a marketing organization has a product its target market wants and a promotional program of value to the trade, it's in everyone's best interest to work together in a partnership relationship to uncover and achieve shared objectives.

Physical Distribution Objectives

The objectives of a distribution system are to minimize costs and inventory levels while simultaneously maximizing customer service and satisfaction. Those two objectives, unfortunately, operate at cross purposes and must be balanced. Whether you are a producer or a retailer, you must balance the cost of carrying inventory vis-à-vis the cost of lost sales or reduced customer satisfaction from not carrying every conceivable product item in stock at all times. About once every year or two a local auto dealership needs a thousand-dollar computer panel for one of its models. It makes no sense for them to maintain that part in inventory, tying up capital that can be put to better use. In fact, the part is not even inventoried in the United States. If one is needed, an e-mail to Japan assures it's on a plane and in the dealer's hands first thing the next morning. That's a good business decision even though it means a customer might have to live with a loaner car for a day.

There's no way of knowing when a retail customer might need one of those computer panels but you *can* anticipate needs of B2B customers who buy component parts and other materials for their production processes. That permits the implementation of a just-in-time inventory system in which inventory arrives exactly as needed. Such a system, with frequent and reliable deliveries, minimizes storage costs and capital tied up in inventory for the B2B customers, a benefit of value.

It's economically viable to air freight an eight-ounce thousand dollar computer panel from Japan but certainly not a load of coal from West Virginia. However, air freight may have a lower total cost of for high value-to-weight items when you consider reduced expenses for inventory and warehousing. And think about it: would you really want to send a truck loaded with Rolex watches on a 300-mile trip down the highway? In the total cost approach, marketers focus on all costs and risks associated with physical distribution, not just transportation. Shipping by air may be a good investment.

Direct Marketing

Many persons think of direct marketing as synonymous with junk mail and annoying telemarketers, but it's much more than that. Direct marketing is big business. According to the Direct Marketing Association (**the-dma.org**), direct marketing sales in 2005 were $1.85 trillion (Yes, that's trillion, with a "t"), projected to reach $2.49 trillion by 2008. All marketers, even those utilizing traditional channels, owe it to themselves to exploit the opportunities of direct marketing.

Business is very different today for the old-time direct marketers that sold through direct mail and catalogues. Now they conduct their business in conjunction with online retailing, a process far more efficient than physical paperwork or telephone ordering. Some successful organizations—Amazon and Dell come to mind—have built a business model based exclusively on direct marketing through the Internet. But even for traditional brick-and-mortar outlets direct online retailing has become an essential component of the marketing mix.

Recently, there was a very interesting partnership consummated between a leading manufacturer of power tools and a leading home improvement store. Top management of the store proposed that the manufacturer market its line of tools on the store's website. That was the carrot. The stick: If the manufacturer declined the proposal and elected to sell its tools through its own website, they would be thrown out of all stores. Talk about an exercise of channel power and an offer too good to refuse! In truth, there was some doubt whether the store could actually carry out its threat, as the manufacturer had a strong consumer franchise and not without power of its own. Nonetheless, both parties realized it was in their best interest to work out a partnership and not a divorce. The deal was done, another twist on today's world of direct marketing.

Inbound telemarketing is another form of direct marketing that has exploded in recent years. I remember its infancy when I was living in Atlanta. In fact, I can distinctly recall a conversation with a colleague in which we were discussing what an idiot this guy Ted Turner must be to have bought a local TV station and try to make a living with what has come to be known as inbound telemarketing. I also have a vivid recollection of another conversation with colleagues years later when we described Ted as an idiot because he thought there was a market for a cable channel dedicated exclusively to news, CNN, but that's another story. Anyhow, Ted had made a fairly good living in town in the billboard business and then he went off and bought Channel 17, in a day when a large number of sets only went between 2 and 13. At the time "everybody knew" that the news came on at eleven and all the stations signed off the air with the National Anthem at midnight, and "everybody knew" that was because "no one" would watch TV between midnight and sign-on at six the next morning. Everybody but Ted, that is, who employed no live talent, just an engineer in the control room, and didn't much worry about selling commercial positions. Instead, he sold everything from party rings to bathroom cleaners through his "800" number and made a killing. Today, of course, you can't spend an hour watching TV without being exposed to an inbound telemarketer imploring you to "Call Now!" Initially, I was skeptical about the feasibility of selling $1500 exercise machines via an "800" number at three o'clock in the morning, but after considerable research am now convinced that things do indeed look better at that hour.

Though technically classified as "direct retailing," there may be great opportunities for some products through door-to-door selling or a "party plan." I never gave a moment's thought to door-to-door until I met a colleague from a vacuum cleaner manufacturer. He told me how they concentrate on smaller towns where their sales reps can meet the people, a large number of traditional homemakers are around during the day, and folks are willing to talk to a stranger who knocks on the door. Even though Bubba won't spend twenty bucks to put out a new mailbox he'll let LaVergne have the vacuum cleaner of her dreams. Selling door-to-door is not what you call show business but do you want a title or the door or would you rather have the money?

The party plan, made famous by Tupperware and Mary Kay, is generally aimed at female target markets, though the old Tupperware party in the home has expanded to events in the workplace to reach the increased number of women employed full time.

Each marketing organization needs to find its own best way to bring direct marketing into its mix and whatever is right today may be very different tomorrow. Direct marketing is big, growing bigger, and new opportunities keep opening up. Surf around eBay for a few minutes, and just try to imagine where all of this may go in the next ten years.

Issues for Retailing

In this final chapter segment, I'm going to address points on retailing from the perspective of a marketing organization/ That is, the different types of retail operations that might be outlets of opportunity for your products. Choice of retail outlets will be affected by the level of distribution intensity desired and places you wish, or do not wish, your products to be available.

With a strategy of intense distribution your objective is to have product anywhere and everywhere potential customers might be. Such a strategy is common for low-involvement convenience products and impulse items such as pop or snacks. Non-discretionary products such as salad dressing and bathroom tissue, whose total usage cannot be changed, will be marketed with the objective of enticing the consumer to choose your brand over that of a competitor or to increase in-home inventory and negate the impact of competitive promotions. If you buy three 24-packs of Brand A bathroom tissue on sale this week you are likely to be disinterested in a promotion for Brand B next week. By contrast, since consumption for discretionary products can be increased they will enjoy incremental sales when available in non-traditional outlets, vending machines, or when placed conspicuously near the checkout. Thus *intensive* distribution for discretionary products may translate to a considerably larger number of points of encounter than *intensive* distribution for non-discretionary products.

A strategy of selective distribution means that you only desire your product to be available in a limited number of outlets that will give the product special attention and which are consistent with the product's image and positioning. For example, Sony only wants its TV sets sold through outlets with a quality image and who offer service after the sale. Although the corner drugstore sells TV sets, they don't sell Sony and Sony does not want to be sold there. Similarly, you can only purchase Florsheim shoes at the finer stores. They don't want to be seen at mass merchandisers.

Marketers can encounter serious problems if they attempt to expand from selective to intense distribution. To begin with their product image may suffer when it is made available in outlets of lower prestige. Even if product quality is unchanged its position in the customer's mind may be affected. Suddenly the brand that was something special is just another low-price nothing. Of even greater concern, current retailers may not take kindly to your product being available at lower prices in the mass merchandisers. A manufacturer of women's clothing learned that the hard way. Soon after expanding its distribution into a major discount retailer its "better stores" proceeded to drop their lines entirely.

Finally, with exclusive distribution, marketers have their products available only at one, or at most a very few, of the very best outlets in an area. Top-of-the line home furnishings, jewelry, and clothing seek exclusive distribution consistent with the exclusive characteristics of their target market.

Vertical integration is an alternate form of exclusive distribution when marketers elect to make their products available only in their own outlets. You can only get Sherwin-Williams paint at a Sherwin-Williams store.

Types of Retail Outlets

The nature of the product and its target market will determine outlets appropriate for its distribution. Consumer nondurables should attain high levels of availability in supermarkets. However, supermarkets may also be an outlet of opportunity for non-traditional products. The retailer tactic of scrambled merchandising seeks to offer a wide range of these products, often at a margin higher than in their traditional outlets. For instance, I can buy a quart of motor oil for less at a discount auto parts store but the convenience of buying it at the same time I do the grocery shopping is worth the extra price. I noted how rack jobbers merchandise many of these non-traditional products. Marketers who generally do not sell through supermarkets may wish to explore the opportunity, possibly using wholesalers, agents, or brokers who can facilitate distribution.

There have been interesting developments in the marketing of private labels in supermarkets. In the past those products were marketed as family brands and perceived as somewhat lower in quality than their national brand counterparts. Recently, however, many chains have introduced lines of "prestige" family brands, and have marketed some private label products as individual brands. Marketers of national brands will need to pay careful attention to market share performance of this new breed of private label and their implications for squeezing national brand shares and margins.

Among "dry goods" retailers Wal-Mart has re-defined the way mass merchandisers do business, very notably in its distribution center concept, warehousing, and inventory control. Their focus on supercenters, adding a grocery store to its traditional lines, all under the same roof, has placed strong competitive pressure on all remaining mass merchandisers and stand-alone supermarkets. Their channel power is enormous. Wal-Mart has led the way in innovative materials handling and dictates to vendors the necessity of updating their systems if they wish to sell products in Wal-Mart stores.

Department stores do not attempt to position themselves as low-price leaders, as they offer better service and atmosphere in the presentation of higher quality products with selective distribution. Likewise, specialty stores command high margins for single lines or limited lines of merchandise, creating value with high levels of service to help the customer find just the item right for them.

A mix of mass merchandiser/specialty store is the category superstore, such as Sports Authority or Circuit City. I find it interesting that these outlets are often called "category killers," supposedly because they destroy profit potential for other retailers in their category. Nonsense! By now you should know that there's *always* a way to find a differential advantage that creates value worth paying for. Here's a personal experience that illustrates this point. Just the other morning, I discovered that my 20-year-old hot water heater had died. There are a couple of category superstores about ten miles from here that have great prices on hot water heaters. I could have gone over there, bought one, arranged for its installation, and endured cold showers for the next couple of days. What I did, though, was to call my plumber friends and said "I need help." Those guys were out here that very morning and I enjoyed a nice hot shower after the daily run. Did this cost me more than it would have at the category superstore? Sure, but not all that much more. Was it worth it? Absolutely!

High quality private label family brands have been a long-term feature of many dry goods retailers. Sears is famous for Craftsman and Kenmore. Now, you see examples such as the line of Behr paints and stains at Home Depot, private label products of high quality that present the same implications for national brands as noted in supermarkets. Just the other day I was touring through some retail outlets positioned between mass merchandisers and department stores. I was very intrigued to note the pervasiveness of designer label knock-offs and higher-end products co-branded with the name of a well known personality. A line of household accessories, under the name of a diva of domesticity, was being promoted at a 40% reduction from the regular price and a line of children's clothing, under the name of a pop music star, was featured with all the boys' pants at half price. These developments are further indications that in all areas of retailing, private label marketing is threatening the dominance and power of national brands.

CHAPTER 11

Advertising: Building The Consumer Franchise

The next two chapters will address the third of the four Ps: Promotion. This chapter will discuss advertising, the next chapter sales promotion, publicity, and public relations. As we've seen, to be successful any product or service must have a differential advantage other than the lowest price. Marketers must create intrinsic and extrinsic benefits relative to competitive alternatives that are worth the price to the target market. But having a good product is not enough. Prospective customers must find out about that product and it must be available when and where they're ready to buy.

Advertising is a sponsor-paid mass communication about a product or service, a product or service class, or an organization. Although advertising lacks the individual contact of personal selling, it enjoys the major benefit of being able to communicate its message to a large number of potential customers at once.

Types of Advertising

Advertising can be one of two types: institutional advertising or product advertising. When most people think of advertising some form of product advertising usually comes to mind, but many organizations also address their strategic objectives through institutional advertising, which promotes something other than a product per se.

Institutional Advertising
One major form of institutional is the promotion of a company's image. This would be especially appropriate for organizations with negative associations or those that wish to pre-empt potential negatives that might arise in the near-term. Multi-level marketing has historically

held an image of low esteem in the public's mind. To counter that, and to make prospective distributors more receptive to becoming associated with the company, one major multi-level marketing organization has run an ad campaign touting the great people representing them and their products. Paper mills, whose aroma often pervades nearby communities, tell residents about all they're doing to help the environment and take a proactive role as involved corporate citizens. Defense contractors don't sell products to average citizens but they'll run ads about their research and development on the cutting edge of technology, pre-empting potential negative reactions from taxpayers hearing about costs for their products.

Product class advertising, usually run by trade associations, is another form of institutional advertising. One of the great ad campaigns of all time was "Got Milk?," which has been copied and mimicked in a wide variety of forms and applications. Think about it. Every time you hear a "Got whatever?" spinoff, you recall that the originator of that concept was milk, don't you? Another successful campaign was "Pork: The other white meat," that positioned pork closer to chicken instead of beef at a time when red meat was getting negative publicity for its potential health implications. After trade associations promote the product class, individual organizations conduct activities designed to attract specific target market segments to their company's product offerings. Within the milk industry a great packaging innovation was the smaller "chugger" bottles, prominently featured in convenience store cold vaults. These packages helped the milk companies gain shelf space among single-serving beverages and have generated incremental sales from customers who would have otherwise selected an alternative beverage product. Among pork producers individual companies gain best food day promotional ad features with strong point-of-sale presence for everything from baby back ribs to boneless pork loins.

A third form of institutional advertising is the advocacy of a position. You'll see this from the cigarette companies promoting smokers' rights. Presenting their case from the perspective of individual freedom to choose and the right to be free from an oppressive government, themes that play well in mainstream America, the cigarette manufacturers hope to build sentiment against waves of legislation aimed at prohibiting smoking in all public buildings or in homes or cars where a child is present. On a different note, insurance companies advocate the need for tort reform and consistent statutes among the fifty states, promoting the need for more legislation, not less, and universal standards set at the federal level.

Product Advertising

Most advertising, the focus of the remainder of this chapter, is product advertising, featuring a message about a specific product or service. Within product advertising, only a small proportion is what is called direct-action advertising: that which seeks immediate action. A relatively new form of direct action advertising is Internet-based advertising, either on a site or as a pop-up. The advertiser's objective, a direct request for action, is for you to click on the icon and begin the selling process. A related form is spam e-mail. You've likely had experiences similar to mine. If you ever buy anything on line, you're guaranteed to start receiving spam from the marketing organization. Fortunately, most of them have an "unsubscribe" icon to stop the flow, a propitious step if the e-tailers wish to avoid the fate of telemarketers and not be subjected to a national "do not spam" list.

Other forms of direct-action advertising, cited previously, are inbound telemarketing through "800" numbers and the record clubs and catalogues that implore you to call or log on at once.

The majority of product advertising is indirect-action advertising and does not seek immediate action. Instead, its objective is to build the product's image and positioning for future purchases, creating awareness leading toward brand loyalty. Though now becoming less common, product advertising may even say something about the product. So, when you're driving down the highway and see a billboard promoting a brand of beer it's not expected that you'll suddenly pull off the road and into the nearest convenience store or tavern to grab a cold one. When you're watching the evening news and see an ad for a frozen gourmet entree the marketer does not expect you to get up, walk out the door, hop in the car, and head for the store. The effect of the ad will be later in the decision-making process, likely at the point of encounter or with the emergence of a need that must be addressed immediately. Marketers will fail to reap the potential of indirect-action advertising if they over-rely on it to affect the customer's behavior. Indirect-action advertising must be planned in conjunction with direct-action advertising and execution at the point of encounter. An organization specializing in plumbing or TV repair needs a dominant presence in the Yellow Pages. Firms that market consumer nondurables need pricing and point-of-sale materials on displays placed in high-traffic locations. Companies that make shopping products must educate retailer salespeople and encourage them to recommend their products. Direct-action advertising, along with promotion and merchandising, says "Buy me now!" It's at that moment that the marketer benefits from the investments for indirect-action advertising.

Some marketers, heavily invested in indirect-action advertising, may feel they can't afford in-outlet promotions and direct-action advertising. The fact is, though, that they can't afford *not* to promote and invest in direct-action advertising. When someone needs a plumber, they won't remember your phone number from the TV commercial and they won't find you in the Yellow Pages if all you have is a line listing. If you manufacture consumer nondurables there's a very good chance your product is not on a prospect's shopping list or that he or she will be susceptible to a competitor's feature in the outlet. If you market shopping products your items must be well displayed in the outlet and spoken highly of by the salesperson.

Advertisers must be aware of the advertising response function, a measure of target market impact as a function of resources invested. What's important to note in the function are impacts at its extremes of a very low or very high investment. At the low end there is a threshold level for advertising before a campaign has any impact whatsoever. For example, if a firm were to launch a new product with one thirty-second commercial on prime-time network TV, at a cost of $100,000, for all intents and purposes the result would be no different than doing nothing at all. At the other extreme you reach a point of diminishing returns when the target market has been so saturated with your message that nothing can be gained by showing it to them any more. I'm sure we can all think of commercials we saw so many times we couldn't stand them and, in fact, began to openly dislike both the message and the product. There's a minimum level of advertising to get in the game and a maximum level at which money is wasted. One implication of this is that brands with a relatively low market share of a category must spend more, on a per-case basis, to receive comparable results, as nearly the same dollar investment is required to achieve the measured advertising objectives. The investment required for a brand with a 5% share of market is close to ten times as high, on a per-case basis, as a brand with a 50% share. For this reason, and others that will be discussed in the next chapter, small-share brands choose to minimize advertising and concentrate on trade promotions, a strategy that guarantees they will remain small-share brands.

Advertising and the Product Life Cycle

Earlier, I touched on points about how marketing strategy was influenced by a product's place in the product life cycle (PLC). Let's now look in detail at the proper role of advertising at different stages of the PLC. It's important to note that advertising strategy is determined by the PLC for the category, not for the brand. A product entering a category in the growth stage of the PLC must adopt the strategy appropriate to the growth stage. The fact that the individual product is entering its introductory stage is irrelevant.

During the pre-introductory period the organization with the initial entry into the category will ensure that information about the product becomes available in those independent and scientific sources that will be seen by category innovators. Media advertising will begin, at a low level, in the period just before introduction and blitz at high levels upon introduction.

Advertising at this stage should be what is called pioneering advertising, informing the target market about the new product category and creating primary demand, demand for the category itself, not the individual brand. Until competitors come into the market, the category initiator *is* the category, with a 100% market share, and an objective of pioneering advertising is to position the brand as synonymous with the category, a master brand with leadership status. Over time, as the target market learns about what the new product is, the initiator will begin to shift its advertising to more of a focus on the brand and not the category itself. Timing of this shift will be strongly influenced by the time frame in which competitors enter the market. If competition is unable to field an entry until the product has entered the growth stage of the PLC the target market will have been informed and educated about the category, and the initiator can make a smooth shift in its advertising to concentrate on secondary demand, persuading prospects to choose their brand. In the unfortunate situation that a competitor can quickly enter the market, the initiator will be forced to modify its advertising to inform the market of the category and create primary demand while simultaneously persuading the market to choose their brand. Earlier I noted that such a rapid appearance of competition might have a detrimental effect on the profit picture for the total category over the long term.

Unless a category follower enters the market virtually simultaneously with the initiator it will be forced to open with competitive advertising to generate secondary demand, sales to prospects who choose their brand because of its superior intrinsic features—"Our product is better because…"—or by positioning extrinsics more compatible with a segment's attitudes, interests, and opinions (AIOs)—"Buy this brand because you're on the fast track to success and not a blue-collar worker," or "Buy this brand because you're hard-working, middle-class, and not pretentious."

Advertising levels begin to decrease as a product enters the maturity stage of the PLC. For master brands with a dominant market share strategy can shift to reminder advertising for the core group of loyal users. Other brands will continue to utilize competitive advertising, attempting to generate secondary demand by persuading customers to buy their brand.

A common form of competitive advertising having much more latitude now than in the early days of television is comparative advertising: Us versus Them. In the old days, no one mentioned the competition by name and butter was "the high-priced spread." Then, little by little, comparative ads began to show unmistakable hints and glimpses of the competitor they were talking about. Today, it's no holds barred. Products compare themselves with an openly named competitor illustrating the superiority of a bathroom cleaner or the size of chocolate chunks in the cookies. And comparative advertising goes far beyond intrinsic product attributes. Pepsi goes straight to the extrinsics and positions itself as being for people who are young and cool while overtly portraying Coke drinkers as old and nerdy.

By the time a product enters the decline stage of the PLC advertising has been radically reduced or eliminated entirely. Either you have a cash cow supporting rising stars or a dawg to be divested.

Creating the Advertising Campaign

Determine Campaign Objectives
The very first thing that must be done when developing an advertising campaign to determine its quantifiable measurable objectives. In the ad trade this is known by the acronym DAGMAR: Defining Advertising Goals for Measured Advertising Results.

Over the years I've heard many marketing professionals complain that advertising people wished them to evaluate the effectiveness of a campaign solely on the basis of recall. There was a very simple reason why advertising people liked the standard of recall: it was the one result that could actually be measured. Marketing professionals, on the other hand, have a different standard: sales! And they wanted a way to measure the effectiveness of a campaign according to how it affected buyer behavior. Their desire is understandable, but the fact is that it's virtually impossible to isolate the effects of an ad campaign from all the other variables in the equation. Awareness is the one reliable measurement we can get. That's not a shortcoming in the evaluation of a campaign, however. In fact, if a campaign achieves awareness—just awareness, nothing more—it's done its job.

When a prospective customer encounters a product—at the point of encounter, in a non-marketing-controlled information source, or in use by an opinion-leader friend—the thought that goes through their mind should be, "That brand advertises." They need not remember what they saw or where they saw it. Just the fact that this is an advertised product enhances its legitimacy and acceptability.

Soon after advertising has passed the threshold level the prospect may still not remember any of the brand's specific intrinsic features. Reaction to the campaign may be predominantly qualitative, determined by whether the extrinsic benefits were consistent with their perceived needs and whether they perceived the target market was people like them. Hard rock music and young talent skateboarding tells teenagers that this might be a product for them, whereas senior citizens quickly realize they are not the commercial's target market. If the extrinsics fit the prospect's AIOs they are more likely to recall the ad and the brand. If they are perceived as incompatible, the prospect will tune them out and not recall the ad. So, attaining recall implies that the ad has hit the proper chord with its target market.

A typical campaign objective might be something like this: 22% of the target market will have unaided recall, and 35% will have aided recall, of our new product in a telephone survey conducted 90 days after campaign launch. This defines quantitatively what you're trying to accomplish.

Make Creative Decisions

The nature of advertising has changed dramatically from a decade or two ago. Some of the most effective campaigns are diametrically opposite to assumptions of how things "had to be done" by "the book." Let's first consider the traditional approach to making creative decisions, the way many old-timers tell you how to do it. According to the old school you started with the product's unique selling proposition, the differential advantage that distinguished you from the competition. Then, you would do the execution—creating the commercial itself—which communicated the unique selling proposition.

It's kind of fun to go back and look at advertising from half a century ago. At that time, the unique selling proposition was a specific intrinsic feature: Brand A beer steam-cleans its bottles before filling them; Brand B detergent has super-cleaning blue crystals that bring out the brightest colors; Brand C automobile has V8 power; Brand D vegetables are picked at the peak time of freshness. The differential advantage was translated to benefits. The product performs better, saves you time, saves you money, tastes better, is better for you, etc. Then, as the ad people perfected their trade, extrinsics evolved to their primary role: if you drink Brand A beer you'll be a social success within your aspirational reference group; if you use Brand B detergent your family will think you're a wonderful mommy; if you drive a Brand C automobile you will be recognized as a person of high class; if you eat Brand D vegetables you will be a healthier and happier person.

For many traditional ads, the unique selling proposition was in the form of a commercial positioning concept, or CPC, which was executed in a variety of formats, all maintaining its central theme. Among the better known: Good to the last drop; You're in good hands; Don't leave home without it; Less filling, tastes great. However you did it, though, there was an iron-clad rule in the old school: You must start with the unique selling proposition and then do the execution. You cannot start with execution and try to work your way back to the unique selling proposition. Today, that's all been turned upside down. Not only do many ads start with execution, they also often do not address the intrinsic product in any way whatsoever.

I wish I'd been a fly on the wall the day an agency presented its new campaign to a major beverage company, showing a bunch of guys on the phone or in person exclaiming "Wazzzuuuup!" Nothing about the product or what it tastes like, just "Wazzzuuuup!" According to the old school you can't do a campaign like that, but within weeks, what were all the young males saying to each other? "Wazzzuuuup!" And, as with its predecessor campaign the talking lizards everyone in the target market recalled the ads. Not only that, they all knew whose ads they were! That's the essential point to recall. The target market must not only remember the ad, they must also recall it was *your* ad. Back to my earlier point: the target market is aware that the brand advertises, and they like the ads. That's enough. If advertising achieves that, it's done its job.

One of the highest levels of recall of all time for an ad was "Mama Mia! That's what I call a spicy meatball!" I don't remember who ran it, which is precisely the point. Everyone recalled the ad but no one was sure what it was for.

Something else to think about: beware of employing a fear appeal as a central theme as the audience may withdraw its attention and go into denial. A few years back some genius tried a campaign around the CPC, "Where will you be when your laxative starts working?" No one wanted to think about that, inconsistent with the campaign objectives. Insurance companies have learned to say, "Do this because you love your family" instead of "Do this because you may die unexpectedly."

A quick point before moving on: I've described how advertising is fulfilling it role merely by attaining recall and positioning a brand as one that advertises. I've also noted that much advertising today says nothing about the product and deals only with extrinsics. That's all well and good, but never forget: Your product must not only meet, it must *exceed* customer expectations if it is to be successful and profitable over the long term. Advertising can grab the attention of the target market and, if the product is properly presented at the point of encounter, entice trial. Then, if that customer's experience is satisfactory, he or she may tell two or three people about it. But if the product fails to meet expectations, he or she will tell two or three people *a day*. We can readily agree that advertising is a great big game designed to get the target market's attention, have them remember us, and associate our product with their AIOs and aspirations. But let's also be sure we agree that the purpose of advertising is *not* to manipulate and take advantage of the target market. A marketing orientation demands that we focus on the customer's wants and needs. A societal focus insists that we always act in the customer's best interest. At the end of the day, when the customers conduct their post-purchase evaluation, it is absolutely essential that they perceive the transaction as having been a good experience and a good value. Never lose sight of that perspective and the customer may grant you the privilege of staying in business for a long time.

Make Media Decisions

Choice of media will be significantly affected by the nature of the product, its target market, the organization's objectives, and spending constraints. An outlay of over two million dollars for a 30-second spot on the Super Bowl isn't for everyone, especially when you consider that the same investment would put 400,000 cases of product on the retail floor with a promotional allowance of five dollars a case. On the other hand no one had heard of Monster.com until their Super Bowl blitz launched the company into sudden awareness and market dominance. And just as a certain status is afforded for "the brand advertises," so is a certain status attained for an organization that advertises on the Super Bowl. The vast majority of firms, though, living in less lofty marketing environments, advertise within more traditional environments.

Television, being visual and audio, offers marketers the opportunity to show as well as tell. Viewers and see the product and its logo in usage situations picturing beautiful happy people of the target market's aspirational reference groups. Naturally, all these visual benefits come at a cost, easily into the mid-six-figures to create a high quality action-packed commercial.

Prime-time network television advertising can run in the area of $500,000 for a 30-second spot, making sense only for large companies marketing products to wide target markets. Even then the network TV audience is sufficiently diverse that some significant proportion of the audience will be persons not in the target market. Therefore, that proportion of the investment is wasted.

Earlier I noted opportunities for many marketers, particularly smaller companies or firms specializing in products for niche markets, to direct resources to cable channels with narrow target markets. Here's another reason why such a strategy might make sense. Viewers of network television, especially those persons who watch many hours of programming, are exposed to hundreds of commercial messages every day, creating a state of commercial clutter. Your 30-second message may reach an audience of a certain size but there's a question about how much attention members of the audience are paying to each and every message. Similarly, touching again on those extremely expensive prices for Super Bowl commercials, I can't help but wonder how much of the audience is engaged in distracting social interactions that detract from attention to the commercial messages. By contrast, viewers on narrow cable channels like CNBC or The Golf Channel, besides being more inclusive of your target market, are likely to be paying more attention to what they're watching. Getting good recall is more than just exposure to numbers of viewers. You're paying according to numbers. Also consider the quality of message exposure to get the most bang for the buck.

Radio was believed by many to be in its late maturity to early decline stage half a century ago as television emerged as the dominant medium. Not so. Radio is alive and well, particularly for the "drive time" segments when commuters are stuck behind the wheel for protracted periods. Of course, radio is only audio and not visual, limiting its capabilities while at the same time dramatically reducing costs for message production. And since the majority of radio is local, not national, it offers greater flexibility for small firms to advertise in their local market area. As with network television, however, audience attention may be low due to environmental distractions requiring high message frequency to achieve recall. It's early in the game for satellite radio but advertisers need to be aware of its emergence and the implications for the heavy user segment of radio listeners.

Newspapers are another medium that lends itself well to local marketing, though metropolitan dailies tend to be mass market publications and thus of limited value for reaching narrow target markets. If, for example, only 20% of the paper's readers are in your target market, then 80% of your ad dollars are wasted. Print advertising—newspapers or magazines—have the advantage of being able to feature distinct information and detail the reader can peruse and absorb at their own pace.

Cooperative advertising between retailers and manufacturers is a common feature in newspaper advertising. Think of all the supplements in the Sunday paper, where local retailers run full-color multiple-page ads promoting products from a wide variety of manufacturers. Each manufacturer featured in the ad has paid a portion of the ad cost, and in most cases the aggregate of co-op advertising funds cover the total cost of the ad. Retailers will command a premium contribution of co-op ad money to feature a manufacturer's product in the highest-visibility location, the uppermost portion of the first page.

Independently, manufacturers run their own Sunday supplement advertising in the form of free-standing inserts (FSIs), better known among consumers as coupons. I'll talk more about coupons in the next chapter.

In the grocery trade another big ad day in newspapers is the "Best Food Day" (BFD) when the chains advertise their features and specials for the next week. BFD ads are dominated by co-op advertising with chains commanding premium contributions for a manufacturer to attain a dominant ad above the fold on page one. As was the case with Sunday supplements, the grocery trade's BFD ads are, in aggregate, mostly or entirely paid for through manufacturers' cooperative advertising monies.

Magazines, the other print medium, have a higher cost per contact than newspapers, a disadvantage that may be more than offset by its benefits of audience selectivity. Magazines like Men's Fitness or Runner's World have a very narrow target market, similar to narrow market cable channels, so ad dollars are not wasted on readers outside the target market. Additionally, magazines will remain in the home longer than newspapers before being discarded and are more likely to be passed along to multiple readers. Nationally-distributed magazines are most appropriate for larger manufacturers but many local publications such as *Atlanta Magazine* and *Crane's Chicago Business* lend themselves well to local marketers, especially those on the high-end segments.

Outdoor advertising is predominantly billboards, a medium of low target market selectivity. Thus, it is most applicable for products with wide target markets or for providing directions and guidance to help customers find their way to an outlet's location. On the interstates billboards help drivers find their motel and inform them of restaurants and services at the upcoming exits. Many advertisers elect to purchase signage on the right-of-way. You've probably noticed the blue Gas/Food/Lodging signs with brand logos as you approach an exit, followed by directional signs and distances as you exit. Many marketers rely on these in lieu of billboards to attract interstate drivers. In some locations, such as the state of Vermont, the blue right-of-way signage is the only advertising permitted.

Another popular form of outdoor advertising is in sports stadiums. In the big cities large advertisers can target the professional sports venues. Everywhere smaller firms can target fields where sports from soccer to football are played by kids of all ages in the local community.

Many marketers feature ads at bus stops and on buses or other commercial vehicles. While on that subject, consider the opportunities to advertise on your own fleet of vehicles. That fleet may be an opportunity to create a moving billboard that gets hundreds of exposures a day. And if your vehicles drive around in areas with buildings more than two stories high, don't forget to put something on the roof.

The Internet is a rapidly-evolving medium with a wide variety of applications. Early banner ads tended to be direct action advertising attempting to persuade the user to click on an icon and take immediate action. Today, many advertisers recognize the value of banner adver-tising in an indirect mode designed only to achieve recall. Pop-up ads are rapidly achieving an unpopularity rivaled only by telemarketers and are being dispatched by filtering software. E-mail advertising to current customers may have some effectiveness and its cost is cer-tainly cheap enough.

CHAPTER 12

Sales Promotion: The Short-Term Boost

As noted in the prior chapter, the purpose of indirect action advertising is to build awareness and loyalty, creating a long-term consumer franchise. By contrast, sales promotion is designed to complement the other elements of the promotion mix for the purpose of achieving an immediate purchase by members of the target market. In a sense, then, direct action advertising, which seeks an immediate buying decision, is something of a hybrid between sales promotion and direct action advertising.

There's an important point to be noted about sales promotion. Its effects are short-term and over time an emphasis on sales promotion relative to advertising will undermine the consumer franchise and condition the ultimate consumer as well as the trade to buy only on a promotional deal. The result will be a decline of long-term profitability, likely accompanied by a decline in brand loyalty and a diminished perception of the product as having special value worth paying for. In some product categories—the American automobile industry comes to mind—buyers have been conditioned to buy only when there's a hot promotional deal. Implications of that are not favorable for the long-term profitability of the auto companies.

Just as many marketing managers have achieved short-term profits at the price of liquidating the brand by replacing their field sales force with brokers, so have many of them reduced advertising in favor of the quick sales kick that will result from sales promotion. Yes, they will enjoy higher sales this year by eliminating the advertising budget and directing all those funds to sales promotion. However, there are likely to be negative long-term consequences to such a decision.

Possible Effects of Sales Promotion

Depending on the nature of the product there will be different effects of sales promotion activity. Non-discretionary products, those which consumers use in prescribed amounts unaffected by price, will increase their sales during a promotional period followed by a decline in sales in the succeeding non-promotional period. Over the long term sales for non-discretionary products will be the same whether they are promoted or not. Examples are bathroom tissue, detergent, and dawg food. You won't run an extra load of clothes, feed the dawg an additional meal, or make another trip to the john because those products were on sale.

Manufacturers of non-discretionary products often run promotions to pre-empt competitive activities. Let's face it: once you reach a one-year supply of salad dressing you're just not interested in buying more. A great example of marketing as war came a while back when one company was test-marketing new toothpaste. Their competitor found out about all the test market locations and about a month in advance saturated all those markets with coupons and in-store features for their brands, ruining the enemy's market test.

The retail trade loses money promoting non-discretionary products, selling them at prices and margins lower that they would have had without promotion. I know of sales reps who have tried to tell buyers about the tremendous sales and profits they'd enjoy by promoting a non-discretionary product. They only did that once, as the buyer threw them out after pointing out the obvious: The sales and profits of the promo period will be followed by near-zero sales and profits for the several weeks following the promotion. For the trade, the only reason to promote non-discretionary products is as a traffic-builder: get people in the store and hope they'll also buy other items at full margin.

The effects of promotion are very different for discretionary products, items consumers don't require and which they'll use more of when available. I was doing my grocery shopping last Thursday and couldn't help but notice a pair of young men—I think they were students at the University—come upon a large beer display at a very attractive price. They went nuts. They grabbed a couple of 12-packs and put them in the cart, commenting about how those would be for the poker game that evening. Then they took two more, noting that some friends were coming over Friday. They loaded in another two 12-packs, saying something about going to a barbecue on Saturday, and a final two for the beach on Sunday. Off they went, set with beer for the whole weekend, right? Wrong! You know what happened at the poker game that evening. They killed all eight 12-packs and had to return to the store on Friday.

The trade is usually receptive to promotions for discretionary products because they represent "plus" business. The very next week, sales revert to the level of the pre-promotion period.

The ideal promotion effect is for sales to jump during the activity but then return and remain at a level higher than the pre-promotion period. This would be the promotional objective for an innovative new product and would reflect repeat purchases from new users. For a non-discretionary product this would imply that market share had been carved out of the competition. For a discretionary product it would imply an expansion of the product category.

Sales Promotion Budgeting

You'll recall that early in the last chapter I stated that the first step in an advertising campaign was to set campaign objectives. The same step is the proper beginning for a promotional campaign but, strangely enough, many organizations take a very haphazard approach to sales promotion and its budgeting. I suspect part of that is because they do not have an entity comparable to an advertising agency helping to guide them through the process. Large marketing organizations seem to have a pretty good idea of what they want sales promotion to accomplish and what it will cost to get the job done but many smaller firms take a very unsophisticated approach that lacks specific objectives. They base sales promotion budgets on either a predetermined dollar amount per case or a fixed percentage of gross sales, never stopping to consider the likelihood that these amounts are either too small to be effective or excessively large and a squandering of resources. An alternative procedure, not much better, is the competitive parity approach. The competition spends such-and-such a percentage, or so much a case, or this much on trade deals and that much on coupons, so we'll do the same. No one stops to consider whether the competition has perfected sales promotion budgeting, let alone whether what is right for the competition is right for them.

The proper approach for sales promotion budgeting is the objective-and-task approach: What is it we need sales promotion to accomplish and what will it take to get that done? A simple example, dealing with one chain of ten retail outlets: A firm wants to move 4000 cases of product through the chain on a holiday weekend. To achieve that they will need a retail price of two dollars per unit, to get a 100-case end-aisle display in each outlet, and to have a dominant Best Food Day (BFD) ad. The question is how much of a trade allowance and how much in cooperative advertising funds will it take to get that done. The total is what they need to achieve the objective. Then, there's one last critical step. Consider whether the cost of the promotion is really justified. If not, they might be well to reconsider their objective and see what would be necessary to move 3000 cases rather than 4000. In any circumstance, why not determine what would be necessary to accomplish several alternative objectives, then choose the one that appears most appropriate? Such an approach will certainly yield better budgetary decisions than an arbitrary allocation.

Strategic Alternatives

Sales promotion activities may be directed either toward ultimate consumers, such tactics being known as consumer promotions, or toward retailers and channel members, known aptly enough as trade promotions. A sales promotion strategy directed primarily at the ultimate consumer is called a pull strategy: get customers to go into the retail outlet specifically looking for the product and have them "pull" it out the door. By contrast a sales promotion strategy directed primarily at channel members is called a push strategy: "Push" the product through the doors, put it on display, and, as the phrase goes, "Build it and they will buy." Another favorite saying among push strategists is, "Build it high, price it low, watch it go!" Many firms employ a combination push and pull strategy using both consumer and trade promotions. However, a firm's strategic options may be limited by the nature of the product and its competitive standing.

Pull Strategy

A pull strategy, sales promotion activities directed primarily toward the ultimate consumer, may be practiced only with products that hold a leadership position in their category and which have a distinct point of differentiation that creates a competitive advantage. Products that are category followers or are essentially undifferentiated from the competition cannot adopt a pull strategy. Attempts to do so will be unsuccessful. Let's consider why that is so.

Think back to the prior chapter where I described the advertising response function. At that time I noted it cost nearly ten times as much on a per-case basis to achieve a desired level of recall for a brand with a 5% share of market than for a brand with a 50% share. The same principle holds true for consumer sales promotions. Running a coupon in the Sunday supplement costs the same no matter whether a brand has a 1% share, a 5% share, or a 90% share. On a per-case basis, however, the cost of running a coupon for a 5% share brand is ten times that of a 50% share brand. For small-share brands, the relative cost of coupons make them prohibitively expensive. But there's even more to it than that.

When a sales representative makes a call on the headquarters buyer on behalf of a category leader that buyer gives consideration to the fact that the leadership brand will be running a Sunday coupon. The buyer knows that large numbers of customers will clip that coupon and come into the retail outlet looking for the product. That fact will influence the buyer's decision concerning the authorization of display activity and inclusion of the product in their BFD ad. Naturally, there will be other components in the overall promotion agreement, such as some form of allowance to achieve an agreed-upon feature price and co-op advertising funds to share in the cost of the ad. The important point to note, however, is that the buyer will be aware of the impact of the coupon and this will influence demands for trade allowances and co-op advertising participation.

On the other hand, consider the scenario when that buyer is called upon by a sales rep on behalf of a category follower with low market share. The buyer knows that few ultimate consumers will come into the retail outlet, coupon in hand, in search of the second-tier brand. The appearance of the coupon will not impress the buyer and will have no effect on demands for trade allowances and co-op advertising funds. Additionally, there is a serious question about the viability of co-op advertising for such a brand. The manufacturer faces the same problem in costs for co-op advertising that was at issue for media advertising or running a coupon, namely that for a low share brand costs of co-op advertising may be prohibitive on a per-case basis. Furthermore, the buyer may be disinclined to include a category follower in the BFD ad because the brand will attract fewer shoppers and generate fewer sales than a comparable feature for the category leader. Net-net: for a category follower, the buyer will be concerned almost exclusively with attaining trade allowances for promoting an unadvertised in-store feature. At best the manufacturer might get an "obituary" ad: a bold line listing on the interior of the BFD ad. In sum, the category follower will be forced to adopt a push strategy.

The strategic limitations of sales promotions for category followers is an illustration of why it is so important to take category leadership and be positioned as a master brand in the consumer's mind. Leaders like Procter & Gamble, Heinz, and Campbell's have developed a consumer franchise that recognizes their brands and associates them with quality. These companies employ a pull strategy *because they can.* Such a strategy gives them power in their relationships with the trade, resulting in better margins and higher profits.

Push Strategy
Implicit in the last segment is the fact that manufacturers employ a push strategy not because they want to but because they have to. Followers and undifferentiated products have no choice other than to direct most or all of their promotional dollars to channel members. Given the dynamics of trade power and the consumer marketplace there is no way to get out of the rut without finding some way to distinguish their product and take a leadership position in a new segment.

Shifting from Push to Pull
An existing brand that is a category follower or perceived as lacking a differential advantage is unlikely to emerge from its current situation. It will be forced into adopting a costly push strategy and differentiate itself with lower prices, which is not viable for long-term profitability. An or-

ganization facing this situation should consider creating a new product, with a unique benefit of importance to its target market, and generate extrinsic images and associations appropriate to the target market. I've described the product development process earlier in this book. Keep one thing in mind: if marketers can differentiate bleach, aspirin, and cat litter, anyone can find a way to differentiate whatever it is they market.

Consumer Sales Promotions

Coupons

The use of coupons has declined in recent years because of their high production costs and relatively low redemption rates. Less than two percent of coupons are redeemed, most of them by current loyal users. Manufacturers want to reward their existing customer base, to retain that loyalty and discourage brand-switching, but they also want to attract new users, an objective more easily attained with an in-store promotional feature price. A few years ago, several major manufacturers indicated they were going to radically reduce or eliminate coupons in favor of an everyday low price (EDLP) strategy, one which has been difficult to maintain in the face of heavy promotional activity from firms forced to employ a push strategy.

Many manufacturers now try to achieve higher redemption rates by including multiple products under the umbrella of a single coupon. Some companies have employed on-pack instant coupons which, if the checkout people are doing their job, are guaranteed to have a 100% redemption rate. I have doubts, however, that on-pack instant coupons can be as effective in generating sales as a price reduction communicated at the point of sale. Additionally, I just have to wonder how many of those instant on-pack coupons are removed by store managers and employees and cashed in rather than being passed on to the ultimate consumer.

Rebates

Rebates, like coupons, offer consumers a price reduction directly from the manufacturer. However, whereas a coupon provides the price reduction at the time of purchase in the retail outlet, a rebate requires that the customer send for it by mail, usually with a form, proof-of-purchase with universal product code (UPC)—the bar code scanned at the checkout—and a cash register receipt with the item's price circled. Because of the time and postage required by both the manufacturer and the customer the amounts of rebates are generally more than those for coupons, and can go into the tens of dollars or more for high-priced items.

There are two special reasons why manufacturers are inclined to use rebates. First of all, rebates generate specific information about customers that will help the firm build its internal database and permit direct contact with end users. But mostly, manufacturers like rebates because they are an effective stimulus at the point of sale. They draw attention and increase the probability of an affirmative decision. And strangely enough, although rebates affect the buying decision, the majority of consumers never go to the trouble to actually send in for the rebate.

Sampling

No doubt you've encountered sampling, by mail or in the outlet. The idea of this tactic is to permit consumers to try the product risk-free, so it's especially appropriate for high-end products, such as Starbuck's coffee, or items people might be somewhat reluctant to try, like buffalo burgers. Implicit in sampling is that the product has some differential advantage customers would find of value. And almost always a coupon would be included as a further enticement to buy. I know this dates me but I remember the days when alcoholic beverage manufacturers would sample liquor stores in some metro markets on Saturdays.

The pharmaceutical industry is relatively new to consumer marketing but has enthusiastically embraced it in recent years. Their field sales reps provide numerous samples to doctors, permitting physicians and patients alike to experience a product's efficacy before making the commitment of a prescription.

Premiums

Premiums may take one of two forms. The type of premium customers most often think of is a special gift or non-product-related item given at the time of a product purchase. Examples would include action figures from a hit movie, free with the purchase of a double cheeseburger at Hamburger City, or a Beanie Baby given to the first 5,000 kids age eight and under at a Cubs game. The other form of premium is product-related, either an extra value pack ("20% free! Get 14.4 ounces for the 12-ounce price.") or a bonus pack, a form of sampling ("Get one ounce of skin conditioner free with the purchase of a can of shaving cream.").

Manufacturers often create a package known as a self-liquidating premium in which the costs of the premium item are fully factored into the promotional deal and the premium item can stand alone. You might see an offer such as "Buy a Bulldawg Cola T-shirt for eight dollars and get a free 12-pack of Bulldawg Cola." The 12-pack is not really "free." You're really getting it and the T-shirt for the eight bucks. And, if you don't want the T-shirt, you can just go ahead and buy the 12-pack by itself.

Contests and Sweepstakes

The point of differentiation between contests and sweepstakes is that with contests you must complete some sort of task to win, everything from submitting your favorite recipe to guessing the number of Ping-Pong balls in a car. By contrast, a sweepstakes is pure random chance and all you need to do is enter, either by mailing in a form or registering on-line.

You cannot demand that contestants make a purchase to enter a contest or sweepstakes so manufacturers must make accommodation for persons who want an entry form other than the one on the package. By making people request forms by mail—one request per envelope, please—manufacturers minimize the number of entries from persons who did not make a product purchase.

Contests and sweepstakes help make consumers more actively involved with the product, thus adding incremental value to the effects of advertising. Costs of prizes may be far less than traditional media. Consider a top-end prize such as a car full of ping-pong balls on display at the mall. If that car is worth $20,000 it might seem like a very expensive prize for the dealer and manufacturer. Until, that is, you consider what it would have cost in TV advertising to achieve the same level of awareness and recall among the same number of people who will see the car on display and enter the contest.

Loyalty Marketing Programs/Frequent Buyer Programs
Loyalty marketing programs and frequent buyer programs are designed to build a core group of heavy users. We often see them in the travel industry: Earn a free trip with 25,000 frequent flyer miles or stay three nights and get a weekend night free. Such incentives are of particular interest to hard-core business travelers, who can easily generate a free weekend at a nice resort every couple of months or so and who can score a free trip for two anywhere in the world when vacation time rolls around. Most companies let employees have the freebies as a perk for tolerating business travel, though some insist that all rewards earned revert to the company and be applied to future business travel. There remains an open question about the tax implications for employees enjoying personal freebies as a benefit of business travel.

All these consumer promotions are tactics of a pull strategy, directed at having the target market search out a specific brand. Having a category leader in their portfolio offers the organization the opportunity to emphasize such promotions and build the consumer franchise. All that helps the dominant brands remain dominant, fortifying their defense at the top of the mountain.

Trade Sales Promotions

Category leaders and brands with a distinct differential advantage may, and should, emphasize consumer promotions but will also utilize some trade promotions. Everyone else, as noted, must rely on trade promotions. I've previously touched on some of these tactics.

Trade Allowances
Trade allowances can be in the form of a reduction of wholesale price, rebates to channel members, or free product. Absolutely imperative with trade allowances is that channel members do something in return for the allowance, not merely pocket the money and apply it to their bottom line. Generally, reciprocity for allowances is in the form of price reductions passed on to the ultimate consumer and agreements to permit special displays in prime locations at outlet level. Free goods are routinely offered to secure space for new products. A "free fill" stocks the product on the shelves at no cost to the retailer,

often followed by an equivalent free-fill credit if shelf space is maintained for a certain period of time after the new product intro.

Earlier I described a short-sighted tactic of replacing a company sales force with agents and brokers. Consequences of such a decision are very apparent in the process of negotiating performance for trade allowances. There is no way an agent or broker can pay attention to each and every product in a trade sales call on behalf of dozens of items. Furthermore, the agent or broker will not be as effective in attaining performance in return for allowances. Consequently, a trade allowance negotiated through an agent or broker may yield only a moderate price reduction at retail and fail to secure an extra display. By contrast, a committed independent rep is far more likely to insist on performance as a condition for the allowance. Similarly, an agent or broker will often give free goods for a new product and not insist that a condition be incremental shelf space rather than space taken from a firm's current product line. Over time, these actions have the effect of raising the costs, and reducing the return on investment, of trade allowances.

Co-op Advertising

Co-operative advertising is the sharing of costs for print or electronic media. Though classified as a trade promotion, co-op advertising is also consistent with a pull strategy, encouraging consumers to come into the retail outlet in search of a specific product. A manufacturer's negotiating position with the trade is strengthened when consumer promotions complement trade promotions. If a company is running a coupon or conducting a sweepstakes the trade is more amenable to outlet-level activities and more inclined to agree to demands for performance in return for allowances.

Conventions/Trade Shows

As a rule the general public is not allowed to attend conventions and trade shows, which are really industry get-togethers for business-to-business (B2B) meetings and schmoozing. These events are a great opportunity to share industry trends and information and for an organization to offer new product previews. Such venues are perfect places to initiate and strengthen partnerships and strategic alliances.

Product Placements

The tactic of product placements is another example of a trade promotion consistent with a pull strategy. It's very likely that product placements will become even more widespread in the future as TV viewers skip or mute commercials. The great thing about product placements is that they are subliminal, offering all the benefits of traditional media advertising without the viewer being consciously aware of the commercial message. James Bond did not just happen to be riding a BMW motorcycle. The folks at BMW paid a price. And Gatorade cups don't just randomly show up on the sidelines at football games:. A fee was negotiated for their appearance, something more than free Gatorade for the players. Think of it this way: would you agree that the appearance of your cups on the sidelines equals the effectiveness of two 30-second commercial messages? If that's the case, and those commercial spots run $500,000 each, the fee for placing your cups on the sidelines will be an excellent value for one million dollars.

Pepsico always ran a product placement for Pepsi in commercial messages for fast food restaurants owned by the company. Recently that tactic has evolved to the featuring of unrelated brands in the message. An AFLAC ad shot in a supermarket setting features a background which is a solid wall of Wheaties or Downy. Great idea! The AFLAC folks reap all the benefits of their commercial message while partnering with other products to defray a portion of the cost.

Other Elements of Sales Promotion

Besides advertising and sales promotion there are two other elements of the promotion mix: personal selling and public relations/publicity. These elements enhance the effectiveness and execution of advertising and promotion objectives. Let's take a quick look at each.

Personal Selling

Organizations rely heavily on personal selling to market customized or infrequently-purchased products or services involving relatively high risk. In B2B marketing, personal selling is the key to building relationships, partnerships, and strategic alliances. However, even for low-risk consumer nondurables personal selling plays a major role in the marketing mix since most of these products are sold through channel intermediaries. Early in the book I described how the manufacturer of such products is really a B2B marketer whose customer is the channel member. The manufacturer's products don't just magically attain distribution and get a BFD ad feature with an attractive promotion price. A salesperson sold this at chain headquarters. Then, at outlet level, shelf space at eye level didn't just happen and a store manager didn't just haphazardly decide to build an extra display at the end-aisle. A salesperson called on the retail outlet to be sure the authorized activities were properly implemented. The partnerships between salesperson and chain buyer, between salesperson and store manager, made it possible. Unless you market through impersonal channels exclusively, personal selling is a critical element of your promotion mix.

Publicity and Public Relations

Publicity is news about the organization, its people, and/or its products or services appearing as a news item. If the news is positive publicity is tantamount to free advertising, but if it's bad it can undermine all other elements of the promotion mix or the entire organization itself. Public relations (PR) is the management of the publicity the organization receives, playing up the good and attempting damage control for the bad.

In recent years leaders of many organizations have been guilty of unconscionable behavior harmful to customers, shareholders, and employees, contributing to negative attitudes about business people in general. As a result all types and sizes of firms have come to recognize the need to generate good PR. Companies selling controversial products such as tobacco and alcoholic beverages present themselves as socially engaged. Firms dealing in environmentally sensitive fields such as oil and logging publicize the actions they take to be earth-friendly.

Enlightened organizations insist on having a culture in which all employees are treated with respect, free from prejudice and harassment. It would be nice to think this was because it was the right thing to do but there are purely pragmatic considerations. Organizations wish to avoid negative PR, realizing that one big negative can obliterate any number of positives.

To the greatest extent possible PR professionals attempt to maximize the advertising value of company news. If the public is aware of a firm and its products in a non-negative context the effect is as valuable as TV commercials. An example that really stood out a few years back was when the NBC line of brands—NBC, CNBC, and MSNBC—reverted to the use of the peacock logo that had been abandoned years ago. When it was originally adopted the peacock was used to point out that NBC was broadcasting in color, a selling proposition that had become trivial. My first reaction to hearing of the return of the peacock was "Big deal!" But son of a gun, in a short time almost everyone was talking about it and tuning in to NBC just to see the peacock. Their PR campaign created publicity worth millions of dollars.

On the other end of the PR spectrum a cat food company was tagging its ads with the announcement that their spokesfeline would soon be appearing in our area and to watch for details in the local paper. To the best of my knowledge the paper declined to run their "for immediate release" announcement and the appearance of the cat failed to generate free publicity.

Chapter 13

Pricing Strategies and Tactics

Pricing, the fourth and final "P," is not determined as an afterthought or in isolation. In the early stages of developing a marketing plan managers must determine how their product compares with competitive alternatives or how a new and unique product can address a market's needs. Whatever the product or service, all its features and benefits go on the left side of the balance sheet and the price goes on the right side. If you add a feature or benefit to the left side, the question always is: how much value has been created for the customer and what price will it command?

The objective of all for-profit organizations is long-term profit maximization, so the job of marketing management is to create products and services of value and implement a pricing strategy that directly translates to bottom-line profitability. I've described circumstances in which managers found it in their best interest to achieve short-term objectives that were in opposition to the long-term interests of the organization. Top management must establish controls to preclude such tactics and in this chapter I will discuss pricing from the perspective of long-term profitability.

Like every element of the marketing plan, pricing strategy is dynamic. The marketing terrain continuously shifts, necessitating ongoing modifications in product, place, promotion, and price. The "right price" at introduction will be different than at later stages of its life cycle and will be affected by competitive actions in the marketplace.

As they taught us in Economics 101, if an industry is attractive more suppliers will tend to come in, thus forcing prices down. That principle is illustrated by market followers who must undercut the prices of established brands for comparable products. The followers ask: how much can we sell at various price points, and what level of volume must be reached for us to be a viable competitor in this segment? The leaders ask: how much will it cost us to crush these upstarts before they establish a beachhead, is it in our best long-term interest to do that, and will the Feds bust us if we try?

Preliminary Questions for New Products

In the business analysis stage of new product development, managers assess the viability of product concepts and estimate sales at several proposed price levels. Simple calculations estimate total revenue (price per unit times number of units sold at that price) and profit contribution per unit (price per unit minus the variable cost associated with the production of one unit). At higher prices fewer units will be sold, and more will be sold at lower prices. The first preliminary question is: what is the price at which total profits are highest in a short to moderate time frame? Later in the process, it may be determined that long-term profitability would be best served by forgoing short-term profits. At this time, however, management is only is only interested in the best possible scenario to determine whether the concept should be given any further consideration at all. This leads to the next preliminary question: What is the break-even point, the level of sales and the time frame in which this venture will pay for all fixed costs and get in the black? If, for example, the break-even sales level will be attained in two months, the concept appears viable and allows for latitude in the pricing strategy that might postpone the break-even time frame to a point that would still be acceptable. On the other hand, if the break-even point would not be attained for two years, even as a best scenario, questions should be raised about proceeding further with the concept.

The third preliminary question, closely related to the break-even analysis, is: At the optimum price, what is the return on investment (ROI) and how does that return compare to other investment alternatives? It's important to note that you cannot set prices to achieve a desired ROI. That's backwards. You must start with the best scenario optimum price and *then* calculate ROI. Of course, ROI is negative until the break-even point is reached. As with any investment the issue for ROI is the return over the long term for the fixed costs needed to initiate the venture. Keep in mind that an alternative investment is treasury bonds that pay around four percent. If your proposed investment pays less than that, it makes no sense to take the risk.

Entrepreneurs often fail to consider alternative investments of their own time and talents when estimating ROI for a proposed business venture. It's essential to consider the fact that an individual can go to work for someone else with no investment risk. If that person could earn $100,000 a year as an employee the loss of that salary must be factored in as a net cost of a proposed venture.

Remember back in the chapter on new product development when I noted that most new products fail and that the job of management is to eliminate ultimately unsuccessful products as early in the process as possible? It's at the business analysis stage, when the issue of price is addressed, that it becomes apparent that many great-sounding ideas will never generate a satisfactory ROI or may never make a profit at all. Kill the idea then and there, once and for all.

Strategic Perspectives for Pricing

Depending on the nature of the product and the competitive situation, the firm will adopt one of five strategic perspectives for pricing. Experiences in test markets will fine-tune this strategy and determine the precise optimum levels for retail pricing and promotional allowances.

Strategy #1: Optimize Revenue for a Given Product Quantity

In some circumstances, particularly in the short-term, a firm may have a given quantity of a product to sell. Its objective is simple: get as much for it as possible. There is an established market price for commodities. There is a certain size of peach crop this year—how high a price can they get to sell it all? Similarly, the manager of a retail store must sell a warehouse full of furniture in the next thirty days. How low does she need to go to sell it all in thirty—not twenty—days? Likewise, consider the situation for the manager of a motel or apartment complex: what price does he charge to maintain near 100% occupancy, maximizing net profits after direct costs?

I've recently encountered two examples of this strategy. I spoke with the manager of a low-end motel chain located just outside a popular national park, inquiring about their rationale for charging

$92 a night for a single room. He said their pricing was set with the objective that the last room would be sold at 10 PM. If rooms sold out significantly sooner than that for more than a week they raised the price by four dollars. If they had unsold rooms for a week they lowered the rate by four dollars.

On a similar note, a colleague had to make a spur-of-the-moment trip from a local airport to Atlanta, less than 300 miles away. The walk-up one-way fare: $800! He was astonished, and asked how the airline could possibly charge so much. The agent's answer: All our planes are full! The airline set a fee of $800 *because they could get it* and was happy to overbook the flight and compensate a volunteer for surrendering the seat.

Strategy #2: Price Skimming: Make as Much as You Can,
and Make It Now
The attitude of price skimming is similar to that of optimizing revenue for a given product quantity, the difference being that the quantity is not a given. Instead, the objective is to skim the cream off the top of the market, a term meaningless to anyone under the age of fifty. Before the diffusion of homogenized milk as an industry standard, the cream would rise to the top (another now-meaningless phrase), to be "skimmed off" for coffee, leaving skimmed milk behind. As a pricing strategy, skimming sells all it can at an initial price, drops the price a step and sells all it can at that level, drops it another step, and so on.

By entering the market at a high price, an organization can quickly recoup its investment in R&D and other fixed costs, achieving break-even in a short time frame. The strategy is only appropriate, however, for innovative leadership products in the early stage of the product life cycle (PLC) for a category with inelastic demand and little or no competition in a short-term to moderate-term time frame.

A skimming strategy is common for high-tech products. Early personal computers sold for as much as $5,000. I just bought a 31-inch color TV for a fraction of what mom and dad paid for their 12-inch black-and-white model in 1947. The first digital watches were priced in the thousands of dollars, then, quickly, the hundreds. Now they're free with the purchase of a burger, fries, and large drink at

Hamburger City. A very few people, though, just had to be among the first to have a digital watch and were happy to pay for the privilege.

The pharmaceutical industry often adopts a price skimming strategy for innovative products knowing that the market will pay whatever it must and aware there is only a short time window before generic alternatives force the price down. Their extremely high investments in product development necessitate high margins early in the PLC.

Price skimming is closely related to the tactic of prestige pricing. Contrary to traditional supply/demand theory, prestige pricing presents a product's high price as an actual benefit. I was browsing around the Internet the other day and ran across a vehicle that proudly proclaimed itself, "the most expensive sports car in the world," similar to how Joy positions itself in the perfume market. Some of the better lawyers in town collect fees of $500 an hour or more believing, probably correctly, that they'll book more hours than if they charged $100 an hour.

With price skimming marketers target innovators who must have the latest and greatest before anyone else, or target markets who need a product breakthrough now and cannot wait for the price to come down. With prestige pricing marketers position their product or service as being beyond the reach of the vast majority of consumers. In either case, price skimming or prestige pricing, there must be something uniquely special worth paying for by a discerning target market. This summer I watched with great interest as a local soft drink bottler marketed its latest line extension with a price skimming strategy, selling the 8-pack of cans at the price of their other brands in 12-packs. I was talking about this with the manager of a retail store featuring a 100-case display of the stuff and suggested in as many words that a price skimming strategy was inappropriate for a line extension in a mature category and that no one would pay such a premium price. You're wrong about that she told me, we sold an 8-pack last week. I rested my case.

Strategy #3: Penetration Pricing: Sell as Much as You Can Now, and Make Profits Later

The diametric opposite of price skimming is penetration pricing, in which the marketer seeks to maximize initial sales volume with an eye to profits at some time in the future. The anticipation of future profits, which may or may not actually materialize, adds an element of uncertainty to projections for a break-even point and ROI, but market conditions may dictate that it is inadvisable to attempt to reap profits soon after product introduction.

Penetration pricing is a necessary strategy for a latecomer to become a serious player in an established market. By the time a follower enters the fray it's possible that the initiator has already skimmed the top of the market, has reached the break-even point, and is enjoying a positive ROI. With the entry of competitors, as I've noted, the level of promotion will increase and prices will fall, squeezing category profits. Market followers may never get into the black at all.

Penetration pricing may be a desirable strategy for a discretionary product or a product with elastic demand, particularly if competitive entries can be in the market in a short time frame. Leading with penetration pricing ensures quick distribution throughout the channels and domination of shelf space and the likelihood of a very strong market share as the market matures. Perhaps most important, this strategy positions the product as a master brand and category leader in the mind of the prospect.

Penetration pricing may be effective in discouraging competitors to enter the market at all, an effect opposite to that of price skimming, which encourages new entries. However, when and if market followers do emerge, the effect may be destruction of profit potential for the entire category, crushing hopes for those future profits.

Strategy #4: "Satisfactory" Profits: Make What You Can,
but Beware the Perils of Greed

Throughout the book I've presented marketing as the engine that drives the organization toward the attainment of its objectives. For profit-making firms those objectives include the maximization of profits. Now, let's add a caveat: in some cases, the organization's long-term objectives are best served by accepting lower profits than might be attained.

The first and most direct situation in which an organization might wish to accept lower-than-possible profits would be that in which the firm wished to discourage competitive entry. This is implicit in penetration pricing. However, it would also be applicable for a firm considering Strategy #1: optimize revenue for a given product quantity. Consider that motel outside the national park. By maximizing its short-term revenue with a rate of $92 a night this chain is inviting competitors to build a facility in the same area. If that happens, rates are likely to drop, resulting in an actual decrease of revenue between the two facilities combined.

There are other, less direct, circumstances in which "Satisfactory" profits are in a firm's best interest. Consider the pharmaceutical and medical products industries, whose target markets would pay any price for innovative products. It's not in their best interest to adopt a pure-play price skimming strategy since it runs the risk of alienating the public and inviting the wrath of legislators. Their long-term interests are better served by accepting lesser profits than could be attained.

Here's a similar situation that presents a pragmatic, legal, and ethical dilemma. A few years ago we had a hurricane go through our area causing extensive damage. Within minutes after stores re-opened every chain saw and generator in the area had been sold out. Local stores could easily have charged $500 for a $200 chain saw, but elected not to do so because of their interest in maintaining long-term business relationships with their customers. Yes, you might nail me once by charging a $300 premium for a chain saw, but I'll never buy anything here again and I'll tell three people a day about you. The resultant situation, though, was that no chain saws or generators were available anywhere in the area and there were no prospects of any coming in for another week. Seeing an opportunity some enterprising guys went up to Montgomery, bought a pick-up full of chain saws and generators, drove them back, and offered them at premium prices. Some local citizens labeled these guys predators and price gougers and shut down their business, an action I considered unwise. Yes, $500 is a lot of money for a $200 chain saw but no one was forcing anyone to buy one at that price. If the chain saw was worth that price at that time—place and time utility—a prospect could elect to buy. If not, they were free to walk away from the deal. Most important, though, was the fact that a market for $200 chain saws at $500 would provide an incentive for other guys to go up to Jackson and bring them back to sell for $450. The market at work! Pressuring an organization to sell at low prices is a disincentive that may result in no goods being available at all! When levels of "satisfactory profits" are imposed by outsiders or regulators, the ultimate result may be detrimental to firms and customers alike.

Strategy #5: Status-Quo Pricing: Follow the Leader
Status-quo pricing may be tantamount to the abdication of a pricing strategy. It is often adopted by smaller players in a market who must react to pricing of the leaders. Consider the auto, steel, or airline industries. One of the leaders announces a price change and everyone else immediately follows suit. On a smaller scale I've noticed it in the neighborhood where the chicken store makes a change in its gas prices followed within twenty minutes by a price-match at the convenience store two blocks up the road.

Another form of status-quo pricing is retailers matching advertised specials. When one of the mass merchandisers features a coffee-maker at a hot price the competitor drops its price on the item to seven cents less. A variation of this tactic requires that the customer bring in a competitor's ad to receive a comparable price.

Special Pricing Tactics

Within the context of any of the noted pricing strategies marketers and retailers may employ a number of special tactics. Here are some of the most common ones.

Loss Leader Pricing
This tactic, generally used by retailers, prices select products below cost to attract customers to the outlet where, hopefully, they will buy other items at full margin. This is the essence of the Best Food Day (BFD) ad. According to the letter of the law it is illegal to sell below cost, an issue I will address in the final segment of this chapter. However, I know of no case in which this regulation has been enforced for BFD specials.

Captive Pricing
The objective of captive pricing is to entice you into a segment where you are captured as an ongoing customer. This tactic was very successful in the early 50s when paper towels were a new category. Some

smart marketing people offered a free two-dollar paper towel holder with the purchase of one forty-nine-cent roll of paper towels. Such a deal was too good to turn down and households all over America took advantage of the offer. What happened, of course, was that the roll of paper towels ran out, leaving the holder empty. Couldn't have that, of course, so all the customers had to go out and buy endless numbers of rolls of paper towels to keep the holder full.

Today, the tactic has been updated to sell you the printer super cheap and make the money on the ink cartridges, or to give you the razor for free and make the money on the blades. On my desk is an excellent example of penetration pricing/captive pricing. A second-tier manufacturer of razors and blades has one coupon for a free razor alongside another coupon for five dollars off a pack of blades for the new four-blade shaving systems. For a secondary brand, this is the way to go: shift the total market to the four-blade system, in which they achieve a relatively high market share, and just hope the day will come when they hit the break-even point.

Price Bundling
The idea behind price bundling is to package a number of items together and price them so that it makes more sense to buy the entire package than to purchase just what you want a la carte, if you can even buy items separately at all. With this tactic high-tech companies sell you packages of their software at a fraction of the cost of buying programs separately. On a personal level, there are no more than five or six cable channels I have any interest in and more than that which I specifically do not want, but I have no choice other than to buy the expanded basic service.

Pricing in the Transportation Costs

Like all product costs, transportation is ultimately paid for by the consumer. Marketing firms factor in transportation costs as part of the cost of goods sold, usually charging higher prices in locations requiring greater expenses for transportation. Competitive alternatives, however, may limit an organization's ability to recoup those additional costs. For example, a firm in Miami is likely to have a cost disadvantage delivering finished product to Seattle compared to a local manufacturer who will incur minimal transportation costs. Market conditions, however, may preclude the Miami firm from charging a price higher than the local competitor and thus it may be forced to accept lower margins or consider the alternative of investing in production facilities at a closer location. In any case, pricing in the transportation costs should be done in the least complex manner possible, making it simple to administer and easily understood by the customer. Here are some of the more common tactics for doing that.

Uniform Delivered Pricing

A policy of uniform delivered pricing offers the same price to all customers everywhere, regardless of location. This is the pricing for a First Class letter, which you can send to Anchorage for the same price as to your next door neighbor. Similarly, it's the tactic employed by direct marketers who charge shipping and handling based solely on weight or the amount of the order. Such pricing may also be noted as "freight prepaid" or "freight absorption pricing," indicating that a firm's transportation costs are allocated across all products as a cost of goods sold. Such a system is extremely simple and appropriate to circumstances such as those of the prior paragraph where it is impractical to recoup higher transportation costs.

Zone Pricing

Zone pricing addresses the issue of differences in shipping costs to more remote locations but, to maintain simplicity, does so by dividing the country into a manageable number of areas and charging different delivered prices in each area. This is the pricing policy for packages delivered by the Post Office or private shipping companies who will charge considerably more to ship to Anchorage than to your next door neighbor.

Basing-Point Pricing

Under basing-point pricing a firm selects one or more places as bases and charges delivery from those no matter where product is actually shipped from. A common example is to charge all shipping and handling from a company's nearest distribution center. Customers in

Pensacola are charged shipping from the nearest warehouse, Houston, even if some items are actually shipped from Bangor. That's a good-for-the-customer example. A contrast would be to charge shipping from a particular basing point even when the product was sent from a closer location. When I ordered the Cutlass in 1979 I was living in Chamblee, Georgia, and had to pay shipping from Detroit, a charge of $283, even though the car was going to be built in Doraville, the next town over. I proposed to save the charge by picking it up in Doraville but the dealer said no, the car would not be drivable when it left the plant. No problem, I said, I'll get some of the guys from the rugby team and we'll push it to Chamblee. They still wouldn't go for it and I was stuck with the shipping charge, which amounted to about seventy dollars a mile.

Legal and Ethical Issues in Pricing

Finally, there are legal and ethical points to be considered in pricing. I summarize these as items of concern and emphasize that any questions should be discussed with your attorney.

Bait-and-Switch Pricing

The unethical tactic of bait-and-switch pricing has been around seemingly forever: entice the customer to come into an outlet with the promise of a bargain that seems to be too good to be true, which it is. The ad features a forty-inch color TV for $99 but when you get to the store you find none left in stock or discover all their screens are broken. The salesperson, however, is more than happy to guide you toward something he assures you will be just what you're looking for. I recently encountered this tactic at a motel outside Denver, advertising a rate of $19.99 on numerous billboards heading into town. What they didn't say was that there was *one room* at that rate, sold out for months in advance, and that the cheapest rate for an available room was $65.

Variations of this scam include the phrase, "Some items one of a kind," which means there is one such item in one store, located in suburban Toledo, and, "Subject to prior sale," which means there are no such items available anywhere but the store manager sold one at that price three months ago to his brother-in-law.

There is only one thing to do if someone tries to old bait-and-switch on you: Turn around, walk out the door, never go back, and tell three people a day.

Unfair Trade Practices

Numerous states have unfair trade practice laws, generally with no enforcement provisions, that prescribe minimum overall margins for wholesalers and retailers and prohibit selling below cost. Such laws are the offspring of the "Fair Trade" laws of the 1930s, which didn't promote fair trade at all but mandated the retail price of manufactured products and prosecuted retailers selling for less. On the other hand, predatory pricing, specifically designed to drive competitors out of business, is a violation of the Sherman Anti-trust Act and will bring on the Feds in the form of the Federal Trade Commission (FTC).

It's often hard to say where good, clean war in the marketplace ends and predatory pricing begins. It's definitely predatory pricing if, as in the Standard Oil scenario of a century ago, an oil company believes it has the resources to outlast everyone else and prices gasoline at twenty-five cents a gallon until all the competitors file for bankruptcy. But most day-to-day situations, even in battles of cutthroat competition, are not as clear cut.

Price Discrimination

Differential pricing—charging different customers different prices for the same item—is illegal according to the Robinson-Patman Act and can *really* anger the party that paid the higher price, who is bound to find out about it sooner or later. However, there are ways to comply with the letter of the law and still address different pricing profiles in various outlets.

No one expects to pay the same price for a product at a convenience store as at a mass merchandiser or supermarket, so marketers do not wish to offer the same promotional deals in all outlets. They can avoid problems of price discrimination through the use of quantity discounts and performance requirements such as a 400-case display in place for two weeks. Additionally, marketers can offer rolling promotions. That is, they need not offer all retailers the same promotion in any one period but may roll the offer through all retailers over several periods.

Thus, the marketer can promote through one big account on Memorial Day, another big account on Labor Day, a third big account over Christmas, and promote through smaller accounts on non-peak times.

Price Fixing

Price fixing, in which two or more firms conspire to set prices, is a violation of the Sherman Act and enforced by the FTC. Such violations need not be open and flagrant, as in retailers and distributors meeting to agree not to promote tobacco products. Even social contact, such as competitors playing a round of golf together, could raise speculation about a conspiracy in subsequent pricing changes.

In sum, there are numerous potential pitfalls concerning pricing and the law, and these are made worse with nebulous standards and circumstantial evidence. Be careful to follow the letter of the law and act as though all your words and actions are being videotaped 24/7. Then, yes, do run it by your attorney.

EPILOGUE
It's Time for the Performance

You now have a picture of the essence of marketing and the instruments of its orchestra: product, place, promotion, and price. All of them are interconnected and must be in sync, satisfying the needs of their target market by creating and delivering value worth paying for.

I began this book by noting the increased competitiveness of the business world and cost pressures faced by all organizations. Expect that environment not only to continue but to intensify. Right around the corner is someone who will produce the same product for less or do your job for less.

But instead of becoming defensive and reactive, accepting lower profits for your organization and less compensation for yourself, become innovative and proactive. That's what leadership is all about and, as you've seen throughout this book, it's the market innovators who benefit from the position in the customer's mind, who seize the opportunity, and who reap the profits before a segment becomes cluttered with competitors.

Find a target market with unique needs you can satisfy uniquely. Build your marketing plan from the ground up and never lose sight of implementation and execution. Take care of your customers. Make a whole lot of money!

Good luck and good marketing.

Bob Kimball
Pensacola, Florida

Index